PREACHING
AT THE
PARISH COMMUNION

3

ON SAINTS' DAYS
AND HOLY DAYS

D. W. Cleverley Ford

LONDON
A. R. MOWBRAY & CO LTD

Printed in Great Britain by
Alden & Mowbray Ltd
at The Alden Press, Oxford

SBN 264 65574 5

First published in 1969

PREFACE

This third volume completes the series on preaching at the Parish Communion which I was invited to undertake by the publishing department of Messrs. A. R. Mowbray. It consists of sermon outlines for the Saints' Days that are included in the *Book of Common Prayer*. And in order to make the book of about equal length with its two predecessors, I have provided material for both Gospel and Epistle for each of the days. The only days I have omitted are some in Holy Week when it seemed unlikely that a sermon would be preached.

Once again I should like to express my appreciation of the encouragement given by Canon William Purcell, Mowbray's literary adviser. The sale of the previous volumes and the reviews that have appeared in the press have also inclined me to think that practical tools for sermon preparation such as these are not without value to clergy whose own inspiration can be so easily crowded out by overwork and routine. The typescript was produced from my manuscript by Mrs. J. Hodgson as was the case with my other books in this series; and Mowbray's printers are to be congratulated on providing a clear and attractive format. Permission has been granted by the Oxford and Cambridge University Presses to make use of the New English Bible, New Testament copyright 1961. May I express my appreciation for all the help given.

Kensington 1968   *D.W. Cleverley Ford*

ACKNOWLEDGEMENTS

The thanks of the author and publishers are due to the following for permission to quote extracts:

Chatto and Windus Ltd., 'Death of a Son' from *Poems New and Selected* by Jon Silkin; Fontana Paperbacks, *Faith in a Secular Age* by Colin Williams; Society for Promoting Christian Knowledge, *The Humanist-Christian Frontier* by Geoffrey Heawood.

CONTENTS

INTRODUCTION

Homely Preaching

The assumption which properly underlies thought concerning preaching at the Parish Communion is that of the parish priest nurturing those whom he has gathered around the Lord's Table. It governs both the form and content of such preaching.

The first implication of this is that he knows these people. A proportion of them he will probably have prepared for confirmation. A number will be active members in the Church's life. Families will be present whose children attend the local school. And so the situation for the Parish Communion preaching is that of a community which recognizes, and accepts with sympathy, their father in God; a community willing not simply to listen to sermons, but to hear what he, their own spiritual adviser whom they know, and let us hope, love, has to say to them. Because of this situation, Parish Communion preaching can be described as homely preaching. Through it the father in God teaches (note the word), God's children in God's house.

Parish Communion preaching, therefore, will be an educative exercise. The preacher in this setting will be anxious for the deepening of the understanding of the faith which his hearers profess to accept. There will be certain aspects of the Church's teaching expressed in the Creeds he will be keen to inculcate. He will be concerned about the balance of their knowledge, and that they should understand what they are doing in their acts of public worship. The Parish Communion preacher will almost have a syllabus in his mind. He will try to cover certain ground. He will keep close to the Prayer Book and the Christian year.

It is this father teaching the family gathered at the Lord's Table which suggests calling the sermon work homely preaching. It means in practice that there will be nothing about it suggesting oration. The preacher may not even use the pulpit.

He may stand on the chancel steps, or if there is a central altar, then in front of it with the people sitting around him.

Because, however, Parish Communion preaching is homely in the sense described, a great mistake would be made if it were assumed that severe discipline in preparation and in delivery were not required. On the contrary, because of its very nature, extra care is necessary for this type of preaching.

For one thing, the Parish Communion sermon must be short. The reasons are obvious. A short sermon, however, that has content and also is able to be received and digested, requires considerable skill on the part of the preacher. It is here that aim and shape, and those other fundamentals of sermon construction described in volume I of this series, must come into play.

In addition, the preacher at the Parish Communion must so possess a grasp of his material that he can present it to his hearers almost without a manuscript, and if possible without notes. The smaller the congregation, the smaller the Church, the more important does the freedom from *aides-mémoire* become. Family Communion preaching must appear to be what it is, the father in God at home in the Christian family. This suggests freedom, ease and a complete lack of anything approaching a paper being read. The preacher's material, therefore, must be shaped so that he can easily remember it (and if the preacher cannot, how can the hearers?), which is the reason why the sermon outlines in this book are divided up with headings.

Furthermore, great care must be taken not to make preaching which is homely, childish. A good school teacher does not talk childishly. Granted the form of his speech is childishly simple, but what he is doing is exercising consummate skill in using language in a simple way. Time and patience are required to learn this skill, but the preacher cannot be excused from attending to it.

In this preaching as in all preaching, homely illustrations are important, if not essential. Pie Duployé in his book *Retorik und Gotteswort* (1957—page 3), writes, 'You do not speak to men with ideas, you speak to them with images. Ideas provide clarity, but images move men closer to them.' The best illustrations derive from the contemporary situation in which both preacher and hearers live. They must be recounted vividly. Jesus was a master in this and valuable lessons could be learnt from the Gospel paradigms. Their stylistic forms are fantastically modern, being comparable to film 'close-ups', and particularly suited to eyes conditioned by television. Moreover, the way in which the Evangelists, particularly St. Luke, vivify their narratives with direct instead of indirect speech is striking. The late Dean of Lincoln, in a valuable book on preaching at the Parish Communion (*Great is my Boldness* Darton, Longman and Todd, 1968), takes pains to stress this.

It is true, of course, that preaching at the Parish Communion, like all preaching, needs to avoid ecclesiastical jargon. The form of speaking must be contemporary, but not slang, for this can so easily and unexpectedly cease to be contemporary. It must use ordinary, straightforward English, in which there is a complete absence of clichés and pious phrases. It is a mistake, however, to rush to the opposite extreme and abjure Biblical language in the sense of quotations from the Bible. It is easy to wax hot against the 'language of Zion' as it is dubbed, and to fulminate about its irrelevancy. Strangely enough, however, the 'language of Zion' is 'salvation language'. The unique message of the Bible had to be provided with a unique carrier. Adaptation was impossible. The word for 'love' is a case in point. A rare word had to be pressed into service—*Agape*. There must be a divine language. The Church's struggle with the Gnostics in the second century was partly about this. What all this means in practice is that the preacher must learn how to quote the Bible verbatim, and without consulting either his notes or the Biblical text itself. Newspaper reporters and columnists know how and when to quote the Bible. What they do in an amateur way, preachers should do in an expert way. Effective Biblical quotation can be electric.

Because Parish Communion preaching is homely preaching, the preacher will not scorn sometimes to speak of himself and his own experiences. Rudolph Bohren writes in *Preaching and*

3

Community, 'To speak of oneself [in the pulpit] is an act of companionship, of solidarity with one's listeners, and therefore also an act of humility.' Preachers must never forget that 'preaching' is a human word, it represents totally human speech, and it is so because the Word of God humbled himself and became flesh. Preachers must be encountered as men of flesh and blood; not as shadows on a screen, as play actors or paper men. Blood must course through their veins, and it will if they are strong and healthy in body. Preachers are their own tool. And if the preacher discovers resentment gaining ground in his own heart because preaching is represented as an art, and preaching short sermons at the Family Communion as a peculiarly difficult art form, he should remember that it is part of the condescension of the Word of God that the preached Word should be a human activity.

Preaching at the Parish Communion is not the only place for preaching, nor the form it calls for the only form. There is preaching which cannot be homely; preaching which must be occasional in the sense that it is geared to an occasion, be it some national situation or local concern; preaching to a mixed multitude, say in a Cathedral; preaching to an audience of students which questions every assumption; preaching to provoke questions, preaching apologetically, dialogue preaching. . . . If preaching is restricted to the Parish Communion its potentiality will neither be developed nor will it be adequately assessed. Preaching at the Parish Communion must be understood for what it is, and what it is not. It is *one* application of the general New Testament exhortation to preach the Word.

In all preaching at the present time the sharpest problem concerns history. It comes to a head over the historical Jesus. Under the influence of Bultmann there has arisen a movement in the direction of discounting history. Existential interpretation has been used to correct the irrelevance which seems to result for the scriptures whenever the historical–critical method of exegesis is dominant. Bultmann's aim is laudable, it is to proclaim the living God, but the God of today must also be the God of yesterday, otherwise the present is emptied of

4

meaning. The point of presenting history in preaching, therefore, Biblical history and above all, the historical Jesus, is not to impart historical knowledge, but to bring about a new awareness of God in the present, which, in itself, is a new act of God, an act by which both the past and the present may be understood. Preaching must learn afresh how to handle history, it cannot continue merely with the existential, above all, it needs to rediscover the historical Jesus.

Such academic concerns may seem a far cry from the homely preaching at the Parish Communion. The preacher, however, needs his own supports independent of the congregation. He must have confidence if he is to preach. He must know that he is acting rightly in telling and retelling the old, old story, in proclaiming Jesus of Nazareth as the Christ, and in using the Biblical narratives as his stock-in-trade. The preacher, in fact, if he is to exercise pastoral care needs himself to experience pastoral care; what is more, he will exercise it the better for having experienced it. No preacher, no pastor, no father in God, can remain in self-sufficient isolation. Even Jesus on the way to the cross needed pastoral care. It is with thoughts such as these in mind that this book, indeed the whole trilogy, is offered to clergy. The primary aim is not to make sermon preparation easier, and perhaps thereby cheaper, it is to minister to clergy, as they minister to others, through the pastoral work of preaching.

SAINT ANDREW'S DAY

The awakener

Romans 10.17 (NEB) *'We conclude that faith is awakened by the message, and the message that awakens it comes through the word of Christ.'*

INTRODUCTION

The parents were worried. Charles, their younger son, could not settle. First he tried a job in the City. Next it was training at a Police College. This was followed by a spell of commercial photography. Nowhere, however, did Charles settle. Then one night he was taken to the 'Old Vic'. His parents did not think he would 'sit it out'. They reckoned he would be 'bored to tears'. But they were wrong. Something happened to Charles at the 'Old Vic'. All next day he could not stop talking about the play. Hamlet and the Elizabethan English seemed to have set light to something inside him. Not long after, he obtained a job on the stage, only an insignificant job, but it lasted. Now he is doing quite well in the theatre.

1. *Faith is awakened*

Faith is like that gift of acting lying dormant in Charles. Until it was sparked off not even his parents knew that it existed. 'We never thought he had it in him' they confessed But Shakespeare 'did it'.

Too often we reckon faith is something which can be inserted, perhaps by Christian education or by the routines of Church discipline. Faith, however, is not *put into* a person. It is *drawn out* of a person. It lies hidden waiting to be awakened.

The Christian home, the Christian education, the Church discipline are not useless. They form the stage, the 'Old Vic', so to speak, where the sparking off may take place, but they are not the same as the spark. Neither do they make the spark. All they do (it is a big 'all'), is help to make the spark possible. They provide for the awakener.

2. The message is the awakener

Charles was awakened not by the stage sets, the curtains or the stalls, but by what took place there. The thing that awakens faith is the message proclaimed in the Christian home, school and Church. It may be directly derived from reading a book, watching a play or hearing a sermon. The means are secondary. What matters is the message. The message is the awakener.

Does the Church wish to evoke faith? Then it must make sure that the awakener is present. The home, the school, the Church contribute to the formation of people; it is the message however, that contributes to *trans*formation. Or, in theological terms, first comes the Law, then comes the Gospel.

3. The word of Christ makes the message

What is the message? Quite simply it is Christ, the word which is Christ. Christ is what God says to the world. Christ is what God is doing in the world. When Christ is made real to men, that is, when he is realized, when he is made living again, resurrected, faith is sparked off. Christ makes the message and the message makes for faith. The Church's first word then is to proclaim Christ, to proclaim him by living the Christian way, by doing Christian works and by speaking about him. Then the awakener is at work in the world. So faith is evoked, drawn out of those who hear. 'Faith cometh by hearing' as the Epistle for today expresses it.

CONCLUSION

St. Andrew is important because he so presented Christ to his brother Peter that faith was awakened in him. St. Andrew is important because he assisted the awakener at work.

Does the Church today really give the awakener priority? Or does it give that place to organization? And what about our own local church? Is the thing which the Sacraments proclaim, the broken body and outpoured blood of Christ, what we really believe to be the awakener of men? What place do we give to the work of St. Andrew? What priority do we give to the proclamation?

7

SAINT ANDREW'S DAY

Introductions

> Matthew 4.18 (NEB) *'Jesus was walking by the Sea of Galilee when he saw two brothers, Simon called Peter and his brother Andrew, casting a net into the lake; for they were fishermen.'*

Have you got a brother? Have you got a sister? Brothers don't always agree with brothers, nor sisters with sisters. Sometimes one sister marries more glamorously than the other, and there is jealousy. Sometimes a brother rises so high in the world that he receives many decorations and a great distance develops in consequence. These gaps do not come about readily in simpler societies, so it is not surprising to discover in the passage of scripture from which my text is taken two sets of brothers working together on the same lake. Peter and Andrew, James and John. This happens in small trading communities. Those of us who know the east coast from Aberdeen to Lowestoft could picture a notice board by the tackle sheds, 'Zebedee Brothers. Boatbuilders, Capernaum', and the assistants referring to Mr. Peter and Mr. Andrew, at least, when they were listening!

But Andrew had cause to be envious. He was a disciple of Christ before Peter. Humanly speaking, had it not been for Andrew, Peter would never have been an Apostle at all. The fourth Gospel sets the facts down in black and white, perhaps in order that there should be no misunderstanding from the other three. 'One of the two who followed Jesus after hearing what John said was Andrew, Simon Peter's brother. The first thing he did was to find his brother Simon. He said to him, "We have found the Messiah. . . ." He brought Simon to Jesus. . . .'

I don't know who was the better of these two brothers, Andrew or Peter. Peter certainly received all the limelight, the commendation and finally the elevation. When you go to Rome it isn't the Church of St. Andrew that dominates the city, in fact I don't even know where it is. There must be one. No, it is St. Peter's that overtops all. And here in London, it is the Abbey Church of St. Peter and the Cathedral Church of St. Paul. Andrew doesn't even get a 'look-in', except, perhaps, in Scotland. And yet Andrew was the first. Andrew, in a sense, has the primacy. St. Andrew's Day, you will notice in your Prayer Book, comes first among the Saints' Days. This is the last Sunday of the ecclesiastical year. Advent Sunday is next week, but even before that, St. Andrew's Day is squeezed in just to make it first. Yes, Andrew has a certain primacy. But he was overshadowed by his brother. It is Peter's name that always heads the lists of the Apostles' names in the New Testament.

I wonder how Andrew took all this? I wonder if he felt resentful? I wonder if he said to himself, 'It's all very well, I initiated the Apostolic following and I get no recognition at all. And if sometimes I am included as a fourth to the big three, Peter, James and John, I feel it is only because I am Peter's brother.' *Was* Andrew resentful? If so, he conquered his resentment, because there isn't a sign of it in the Gospels. On the contrary, he went on introducing outsiders to Jesus. It was Andrew who introduced the lad with the five barley loaves and the two small fishes to Jesus when the five thousand were fed. It was Andrew who brought the Greeks to Jesus, when for some reason Philip hesitated. Andrew apparently never said: 'I introduced one newcomer to Jesus, and I got no glory, I will never do so again.' Andrew never let himself be dwarfed by resentment on account of his brother's elevation.

There are some lessons to be learnt from all this, and the *first* is to form a true estimate of the proportion of things. Last Monday evening I had to spend three hours at the London Diocesan Conference. A number of competent speeches were made both by clergy and laity, chiefly laity. It would have been very easy to reckon that this was where the important work of the Church was being carried out. It *was* controversial, colourful and clever. Yes, and very necessary. Conferences have to be. But it could be that the *real* work of the Church was being carried on completely unknown where some Church worker was wrestling in some cheap lodging house for the soul of a young woman taking to drugs; or some ungifted clergyman, whose heart was nevertheless of gold, spending the evening with a man from whose life the bottom had fallen, because his wife had died, and there were no other friends that cared. The work of Christ is not only done by the Peters, speaking eloquently in public Conference Halls, but in lonely rooms with thick pile carpets in the West End, or thick flowery lino in the East End. Human hearts are much the same wherever you go. I have learnt that in thirty years as a clergyman. And great work is done by Andrews as well as Peters, though they make no speeches and never seem to earn a note of public commendation and be given any kind of medal. St. Andrew's Day is the day for the unsung leaders in the Christian cause— mothers, undistinguished friends, souls that pass in the night but helped us on our way. Of such and by such is the Kingdom of God made. The unshowy people who humbly do their best even for the lowly, as Andrew did it for the lad with five loaves and two small fishes, and for the Greeks who felt out-siders.

Secondly, I think that the real work of the Church, the real work of a Christian, is simply to introduce others to Christ. This was what Andrew did, and he never let resentment of Peter get in the way. He brought Peter. He brought the lad. He brought the Greeks. Perhaps Andrew was a simple man. Is this why he is always shown in the company of Philip in the lists of the Apostles, for Philip was undoubtedly uncomplicated, if not dull? But Andrew knew the essential and put it into practice. He introduced those closest to him, his brothers, and those farthest from him, those Greeks, to Christ. It made no difference where people stood. He was certain where to bring them.

Would it not be possible at St. Andrew's tide for us as a congregation to learn this lesson and put it into practice? I have noticed how some of you have been bringing friends to church and I have thanked God for it. To bring *ourselves* these days isn't easy, for church-going is out of fashion, but to bring someone else is true Christian discipleship, after the pattern of Andrew. I often think a Carol Service gives us a chance for this. It is so easy to say 'Come to the Carol Service!' but who knows what it might achieve?

You may not be Peter. I am certainly not. But we could, both of us, be Andrew. We could seize every opportunity to bring someone else to Christ. We could see the true proportion of things and how most often God's work is carried out in the unobtrusive lanes of life. And we could resist every form of resentment at another's elevation, privilege or prize. God may have called us to be Andrew and not Peter, but Andrew was an Apostle as well as Peter. God needs the Andrews. That is why perhaps he called him first. Never underestimate God's care for Andrew. Never underestimate God's care for you, Andrew though you are.

SAINT THOMAS THE APOSTLE

No outsiders

Ephesians 2.19 (NEB) 'Thus you are no longer aliens in a foreign land . . .'

INTRODUCTION

One week-day afternoon in the summer I watched a middle-aged man enter the Church and stand for a long time gazing up at G. F. Bodley's magnificent altar piece and then at the stained glass window above it, Finally, he withdrew from their case a pair of binoculars and focused them on the object of his interest. This made me anxious. Was he perhaps prospecting for thieves? Then he made his way to examine a tapestry on the wall. It depicted Christ in the garden of Gethsemane. At this I thought I ought to speak to him. I said 'Do you like the Church?', but I received no reply. He stared at me. Then he said quite simply *'Non capisco'*, ('I do not understand'). In another sense, however, he understood perfectly. Italian he might be, and technically an alien in a foreign land, but the representations of Christ on the Cross and Christ in the garden of Gethsemane which were the objects of his sympathetic gaze brought him close to us, we were joined in the same Christian devotion. We were members of God's household. My last memory is of him looking up at the Church and saying *'è bella! è bella!'* ('It is beautiful').

1. *No outsiders*

As far as God is concerned there are no outsiders. No-one is an outsider to God. This is shown to be so because Christ (and God was in Christ), accomplished his greatest work not in the Holy of Holies in the Jerusalem Temple, but outside even the city walls. What he had to do for men he did on Skull Hill (Golgotha), where the dregs and drop-outs ended, and those who reacted to authority with violence. If Christ went there, and he did, obviously as far as he is concerned there are no outsiders to him. Today's epistle begins (Prayer Book Version) 'Now therefore'... It is because of what Christ did that 'there are no more strangers and foreigners but fellow-citizens with the saints, and of the household of God'.

2. *Response is necessary*

There is, however, nothing automatic about God's action. Christ did not pull a string or press a button and lo, all men were henceforth members of God's household. They had to respond. They had to accept the gift of membership. And it is a gift. It is not the result of qualification. Skin doesn't qualify. Skill doesn't qualify, nor even faith. Membership in God's household is not a *reward* for faith. We cease being aliens to God when we accept the fact that he is not hostile to us. He was not even antagonistic to those who crucified him on Skull Hill. On the contrary, the truth is 'God so loved the world that he gave...'. But we have to respond. Free will is not overruled. God's action is not automatic. Man has a part to play.

3. *Insiders can become ousiders*

Suppose, however, a man has been a recognized member of the household of God, can he become an outsider? He can never become an outsider to the love of God because he never has been, but can he *see himself* as an outsider and therefore shut himself off from the grace of Christ? Apparently this is what Judas did. He was an Apostle but he put himself out. Peter nearly did likewise because there is not much difference between a traitor and a denier. And Thomas stayed outside the inside gathering of the other Apostles after Christ's resurrection affirming 'I will not believe'. In all three cases Christ tried to win them over to the inside. He even offered Judas the tasty morsel at the last supper. He failed with Judas, but he succeeded with Peter and Thomas. They were restored to the household of faith.

APPLICATION

Does this message today address itself to a Thomas? Does it address itself to anyone inside the fellowship whose doubts are urging him to pass through the door to the outside again? Let there be no misunderstanding. Intellectual grasp of theological formulae is not what we are considering. What we have in mind is doubt of God's love. Yes, for individuals as well as the whole world. This is what makes a man put himself outside. And being an outsider always spells unhappiness. So I take your minds back to Skull Hill, to Christ *out* there and remind you that no-one can possibly be an outsider to God in the face of what took place at Golgotha. That is why Paul wrote in the letter he addressed to the city of Ephesus where they used to practise the heathen worship of the goddess Diana: 'Thus you are no longer aliens in a foreign land, but fellow-citizens with God's people, members of God's household.'

SAINT THOMAS THE APOSTLE

What to put first

> John 20.25 (NEB) *'Unless I see the mark of the nails on his hands, unless I put my finger into the place where the nails were, and my hand into his side, I will not believe it.'*

It's a bit crude, isn't it? I mean, we might let the phrase pass about *seeing* the nail marks, but when he goes on to talk about 'putting his finger into the place where the nails were', and, as if that were not sufficient, 'putting his hand into his side', we must confess, we are rather 'put off'.

But this is Thomas, Thomas the Apostle, about whom, if we know anything at all, we know he was a doubter, he doubted Christ's resurrection. We still talk about 'doubting Thomases'

1. *A prosaic man*

I used to let myself fall into the unthinking common opinion that Thomas was a sort of donnish type, the kind of man who splits hairs, and finds it difficult to think straight as ordinary people think; rather like the American who went to Oxford, and when he came back, his friends enquired what he was like, only to be told, 'Oh, he's just like he used to be, except he's gotten so as he can't understand.'

Thomas wasn't like that. I doubt if Thomas had sat for fifty years in some philosophical school he would ever have become a philosopher. Thomas had no flights of fancy, saw no visions, conjured up no theories of existence. Metaphysics, philosophy and abstract poetry, yes and Picasso would be out for him. Thomas was prosaic, and if the truth were told, a bit dull. Twice in the fourth Gospel we find him misunderstanding Jesus, once at the death of Lazarus, and once in the upper room the night before the crucifixion.

And not only was Thomas prosaic, he was melancholy. He is not in evidence in the Gospel narratives except there was a death, or talk of death. Perhaps he loved funerals and graveyards. There are people like that.

But Christ chose him to be one of his followers. That is the first point to lay hold of with both hands. Christ sees possibilities in us where we perhaps see no possibilities. God does not want all his people to be dons, poets and philosophers. He wants business men and shop-keepers, carpenters and housekeepers, though I am quite sure that being a Christian will in the end split open some of their hardheadedness. No man can be a believer in Christ and remain completely prosaic. For one thing, he has to come to terms with the resurrection, and that's enough to split open any prosaic mind. But a man may start on the Christian way just like Thomas, dull, matter-of fact and rather melancholy.

2. *The challenge to prosaic nature*

But then Easter comes. What are we going to do with Easter? What is Thomas going to do with it?

You must remember, Thomas was a devoted follower of our Lord. Openly and before his fellow disciples he declared himself willing to die with Jesus. Life for Thomas would be unthinkable without a Christ to inspire him. He'd rather be dead himself. After all, he didn't mind graves and funerals all that much. He would half like to be a martyr. He was that type.

And here is your business man quite convinced in his own mind that life cannot proceed without Christianity, by which he means teaching men to be honest, clean minded, respectful and loyal, in the absence of which, no business can succeed, nor government policy prevail.

But what about the resurrection? Isn't that going a bit far? Doesn't it spoil the whole movement? Isn't it dragging in a kind of magical, fairy tale, 'will-o-the-wisp' element, enough to drive sensible men away from following any more? After all miracles don't happen with income and expenditure accounts. You know just where you are, and it would be pretty awkward if you didn't.

So Thomas is not going to have any truck with resurrections. Mary Magdalene and the other women can say what they like about having seen Jesus. The whole Apostolic group can chant away till Doomsday that Christ has appeared to them in 'the upper room'. The more they talk, the more Thomas gets worked up, till in the end his protestations are even crude. 'Unless I see the mark of the nails on his hands, unless I put my finger into the place where the nails were, and my hand into his side, I will not believe it.' Perhaps he didn't mean to say all this, but you know how it is, people make you mad, and then you hit out.

Thomas sounds definite. And when people get worked up in their stubbornness, there is nothing else to do but wait till they have 'cooled off'. In time they will come to a deeper experience of life. $2+2=4$ is not the whole underlying pattern of existence. An element of mystery exists, nor is it any use seeking out the scientists to lend support to a philosophy of materialism, because *they* certainly will not give it.

3. *The one thing needful*

But the Lord appeared to Thomas. That is why he changed. Not, you observe, because of the empty tomb. He had certainly heard of it. Perhaps he even went to see where the body of Jesus had lain in the sepulchre, and from which it had disappeared. But the empty tomb did not make him a believer. For that matter, it did not make nine other Apostles believers in the resurrection either. Only the disciple 'whom Jesus loved', as he is called in the fourth Gospel, went into the tomb and saw and believed. All the others needed an appearance of Jesus to convince them.

All this is why we should not be too upset when we hear some modern theologians affirming that the empty tomb of Christ does not matter. What matters is the appearances. I don't suppose there is a single person in this Church who is a Christian because of the evidence of the empty tomb. We are Christians because we were brought up in the tradition *and* because at some point in our lives God has become real to us. It may have been a trouble we overcame unexpectedly, or a joy that came our way, we never dreamed of; it may have been quite a definite conversion from agnosticism, but whatever it was, it was that appearance (if we may use the word), of Christ to us as a reality that made all the difference.

Thomas would say 'Amen' to all this. It is true of me, he would affirm. But this is the point I would like to throw in. After his experience of the risen Lord, do you think he would say the empty tomb does not matter? Wouldn't he go back to it, back to the thought of it, to the place itself, perhaps, and see it all with new eyes, the eyes of faith, and the eyes of understanding? And wouldn't he, being the kind of prosaic man he was, cling to it with no possibility of being shaken?

APPLICATION

This is the point I want to press home from the story of Thomas. In the Christian way everything turns on what you put first. We do not say you must believe in an empty tomb, you must believe that the appearances were actual manifestations of a physical presence and not visions, you must believe in a physical ascension, all of this may come later. Yes, I think ought to come, if the faith is to hold, but first and foremost comes the personal awareness of the risen Christ in one's life. That is where we start. That is where we finish. That is the thread which runs throughout the whole experience of being a Christian from start to finish.

> Christ within me,
> Christ behind me,
> Christ before me,
> Christ beside me,
> Christ to win me,
> Christ to comfort and restore me,
> Christ beneath me,
> Christ in hearts of all that love me,
> Christ in mouth of friend and stranger.
>
> (*Ascribed to St. Patrick*)

That is living the life of a Christian. Let Thomas teach us to get our priorities right, and if we do not think as every other

Christian does, even about basic events in the gospel story, let us be patient. The real thing is living with Christ now, all else is but at best a help towards that final purpose. Living in the presence of Christ now.

I remind you of how the chapter ends from which today's story is taken. 'There were indeed many other signs that Jesus performed in the presence of his disciples, which are not recorded in this book. Those here written have been recorded in order that you may hold the faith that Jesus is the Christ, the Son of God, and that through this faith you may possess eternal life by his name.'

So now we know what is the important thing. It is holding fast, and being held fast by the eternal life now. All else is secondary.

CHRISTMAS DAY

Splendour

Hebrews 1.3 (NEB) '... *the effulgence of God's splendour and the stamp of God's very being.*'

1. *Splendour*

This is 'big stuff'. I mean the Epistle for today. And you need to be a skilled reader to read it aloud in public, because it rolls off the tongue. It is full of pitfalls for those unwary of what distortion a false emphasis can produce. And the Greek is tremendous. Whoever the author was, he must either have worked at it in order to produce this self-conscious literary form, or else it came straight out of heaven. That can happen. In either case it is 'big stuff'. This is Christmas in its full catholic understanding, the justification for copes and candles and magnificence.

2. *The splendour of faith*

But it is the splendour of faith, not of sight. This is not what you would have seen had you been one of the shepherds visiting the manger in Bethlehem on Christmas Eve, nor one of the 'wise men', nor even Mary herself. You would have seen no splendour. Only a smelly yard and an incontinent baby. Some never do see any splendour, not even though they recognize in this child a great teacher to be, a reformer to be, and a significant martyr. But faith sees more, the Bible sees more, the Church sees more. So much does it see, that in an Epistle like today's, symbolic words are positively lavished on his description. The child is 'the Son', 'the heir to the whole universe', 'the splendour and stamp of God's very being', he who sustains all that is by the word of his power, the occupant of the throne of eternity with God himself, far above the lofty height of the loftiest of angels. This is 'baroque' language, the baroque language of vigorous faith.

3. *Faith by the Word*

How has this faith been evoked? The answer is because he who came on Christmas Day has spoken. Others have spoken before, and God was heard through them, *is* heard through them. And God has spoken to some of us through a sunset, the crocuses carpeting a corner of the park in March, an illness from which we unexpectedly recovered, but all these voices are fragmentary. In Jesus, however, the child Jesus, the man Jesus, teacher, healer, sufferer on this cross of wood, triumphant victor over the grave, we hear a voice of another dimension. This is not simply God speaking through a man, the man *is* God's speech, God's word, God's active presence. Not only what Jesus said, but everything about him, everything he did, about the way he looked at people, everything he suffered was, *is* God speaking. Jesus is the effulgence of God's splendour and the stamp of God's very being.

APPLICATION

When we come to the Eucharist today, and Eucharist, thanksgiving is right for Christmas Day, we, like those shepherds will see very little. An ordinary piece of wafer bread, a chalice of not uncommon wine; but the Church asks that we look with the eye of faith, her faith, if not our own faith as well, which is better. What we shall receive is the symbol of the presence of such a majestic being as scarcely the words of the writer of the Epistle could describe, pile them on though he did. Our Holy Communion will be with 'the effulgence of God's splendour and the stamp of God's very being'. I ask you for one moment, pull out into the deep of Christian faith, away from the ordinary, out into splendour, this is what God is offering you, his splendour, his magnificence, his power. Come with this in mind to his table today, come with faith of this dimension. And remember, according as is your faith, so will it be done unto you.

CHRISTMAS DAY

The tent

S. John 1.4 (RV) '*And the Word became flesh, and dwelt among us. . .*'

1. *A tent*

One of the journeys I frequently make by car is across Clapham Common. Twice every year in May and November that common is dominated by a huge tent. It is erected to accommodate Billy Smart's Circus, and judging from the number of cars parked there while the fun is on, it must house a 'roaring trade'.

But it is only temporary. One day you cross the Common and there is the tent. Next time there is no tent. A tent is a temporary erection for a special purpose. This is the distinctive fact about a tent.

2. *Christ's tent*

Now the text I have chosen from the Gospel for this Christmas

Day tells us about a tent. You probably do not recognize this, but the word 'dwelt' means 'tented' in the Greek original. So the text could read, 'And the Word became flesh and *tented* among us.'

Perhaps it comes as a fresh idea that Christmas should speak to us of a tent. Clearly, however, it was Christ's flesh that constituted the tent in which he lived for a short time for a special purpose. The Word of God, intangible and invisible, came and lived among us so that we might touch him and see him. And some people actually did so. It is an astonishing thought. It was an astonishing experience for those who underwent it. These were the Apostles. They talked about it for the rest of their lives. John says in his first letter: 'It was there from the beginning; we have heard it; we have seen it with our own eyes; we looked upon it, and felt it with our own hands; and it is of this we tell.'

In a way a tent life is a rough and ready kind of existence. And St. Paul makes quite clear that the life of Christ on earth was what he calls a self-emptying, a humbling of himself. It is in this sense that we can speak of Christ as coming down from heaven. It has nothing to do with space but everything to do with living on a lower plane, namely existence in a material body, subject to frustrations and temptations.

3. Our tent

We human beings, of course, also live in that tent, and we do not know any other kind of life. Our life is essentially life in the body, or so it seems. But St. Paul teaches us that our life in the flesh is temporary. When we cross the frontier post of death we shall experience life of another quality; that is, eternal life. It will replace temporal and temporary life.

APPLICATION

What then should be our attitude to Christmas Day? Surely one of profound thanksgiving. Christ took human flesh and appeared as the Babe of Bethlehem and the Man of Galilee and Judaea, so that we mortal men might make actual contact with the Eternal. We call this the Incarnation. It was an act of purposeful humiliation for our sake.

And this is what God is like, ever seeking to draw close to us so that our life might touch his life. And when you come to think of it, this is what is happening in the Eucharist. Christ is making himself available by means of the material elements of bread and wine so that we might almost call them a tent. 'And the Word became flesh and tented among us. . . . ' On this Christmas morning what could be more right than reverently and with thanksgiving to draw near to that tent.

SAINT STEPHEN'S DAY

The identity of the child

I would like to tell you about Stephen, about his subtle mind, his comprehensive mind, and his liberal mind; not only that, but his skill in practical administration, and how rarely the scholarly bent and the practical bent fits together, but they did in Stephen; and how the infant Church needed such a giant as this, and he appeared, yet not among the Apostles but among seven deacons, appointed 'to serve tables'. Stephen is unexpected, brilliant and thrusting. He appears like a meteor in the sky, and vanishes as swiftly.

But St. Stephen's Day is not set apart to tell us about Stephen. If we need any confirmation we require only to look at its setting—the day following Christmas Day; and if this is insufficient, a glance to the portion of scripture appointed for the Epistle. It consists of a few verses about his death, that is all. And the Gospel takes up the martyr theme. Why? Because St. Stephen's Day is set to indicate the identity of the child lying in the manger.

Who is he?

1. *A costly child*

He is not an ordinary child, not only the offspring of a young woman married to a village carpenter, he is someone for whom a man of Stephen's calibre is prepared to give his life. This is a costly child, costly in the sense that if you own him, it may cost you your life. Why did men 'cry with a loud voice, stop their ears, and run upon Stephen with one accord, and cast him out of the city, and stone him'? Because he had opened the door of Bethlehem's stable, and seen in the manger, not simply a baby, but one who shared the glory of God in equality. To own that vision is costly.

2. *A King of eternal destinies*

Who is this child? He is one to whom a man commits his spirit at the end of life. 'And they stoned Stephen, calling upon God, and saying, "Lord Jesus, receive my spirit." ' In the hands of God lies the issue of all things. What God is, Jesus is, King of eternal destinies, and the baby's name is Jesus.

3. *The Lord of mercies and forgivenesses*

Who is this child? He is a Master in the following of whom a new attitude is developed in respect of our enemies. Perhaps there is no surer test of a man's earthly significance than that he influences people's attitude in the sphere of age-old relentlessness. The child in the manger was he who came to enable Stephen to say of his enemies while they stoned him, 'Lord, lay not this sin to their charge.' Sin, yes, sin it was, stoning Stephen, but because of the child in the manger on Christmas Day, sin is never the end of the human story. The springs of forgiveness and reconciliation rise up from Bethlehem. The child there wrapped in swaddling clothes is one, the One to whom belong 'mercies and forgivenesses, though we have rebelled against him.'

What is the Church's answer today?

Who is this child in the manger of Bethlehem? Many diverse answers are possible. The Church answers in the *Book of*

Common Prayer with the confession of Stephen's lips. Does it still stand by that confession now? Does it rank Jesus as high as this?

SAINT STEPHEN'S DAY

Anomalies

> Matthew 23.37 (NEB) *'O Jerusalem, Jerusalem, the city that murders the prophets . . .'*

Why does Jerusalem murder the prophets? Why does any community murder its prophets? Why has it been known for the Church to murder its prophets, or if not to murder them, to see that they have no influence? The answer is, because prophets are awkward people, they ask awkward questions, they do not fit into 'the system', they are not complacent about the *status quo*. It was for being such a person that Stephen lost his life. The men of Jerusalem stoned him to death.

1. *Religion versus the prophets*

We must remember that Jerusalem was a religious city. It was the seat of the most highly developed form of religion the world had seen. Through Judaism came the knowledge of the one true God. But religion can resent prophets. Orthodoxy can resent disturbance. Nothing, in fact, worries established religion so much as the suggestion that there could be new ways of looking at traditions.

2. *Ecclesiastical suppression*

Jerusalem must learn to bear with its prophets. The Church must learn to accommodate its innovators. They are necessary to the health of both Jerusalem and the Church because orthodoxy and formalism can be dead hands. The implication, however, is not that Jerusalem and the Church must be handed over to the prophets. If they were, chaos would reign. Prophets do not and probably cannot manage organizations; and organizations have to exist and they have to be managed. We need bishops to keep an eye on Church order, and priests to keep the religious life of the Church tidy; but if the prophets are banished, if the unorthodox are suppressed, if the freedom of enquiry is disallowed, the end is desolation. Such was the fate of Jerusalem. In today's Gospel we hear the sigh of Jesus over this city. 'O Jerusalem, Jerusalem, the city that murders the prophets and stones the messengers sent to her!. . . Look, look! there is your temple, forsaken by God.'

3. *The idol of organization*

Where do we fit into this stern picture? We who are about to kneel at the Communion rail, the fellowship rail. We could feel satisfied that our worship is one hundred per cent regular, orderly and in accordance with the most up-to-date liturgical trends. Is there a wish to see a pattern of what Eucharistic worship should be? Then come to our Church. What a dangerous situation! Jerusalem needed disturbing prophets. A Church needs its anomalies. Anomalies make us think. They make us examine our priorities. They prevent us from settling down and settling down means desolation for a Church. Do not make too much of tidy organizations. It can become an idol and then it needs breaking down. It was the prophets' work to break down idols. This is why they were not popular.

SAINT JOHN THE EVANGELIST'S DAY

The declaration

> 1 John 1.3. '*That which we have seen and heard declare we unto you, that ye also may have fellowship with us.*'

A short time ago there was quite a stir because flying objects like fiery red aeroplanes were reported as having been seen in the sky. Nobody paid very much attention. Of course their were remarks about people 'seeing things', but interest would have died down had not the newspapers recounted how some men in a car had followed one of these 'things' as they drove down a country lane. After which all the urge was to find the men and question them. A rumour is one thing. Testimony to having seen and heard is quite another.

1. *The man Jesus*

And this is why the Gospel which John the Evangelist and his fellow Apostles proclaimed created such a stir. They did not simply come with a doctrine of eternal life. Many people before had come telling of life of a superior quality and how it was to be acquired. It might be by asceticism, by almsgiving or meditation. The Apostles, however, had something entirely different to declare. They said, 'What we have seen and heard we declare.'

Of course we want to test them. We want to know if they are 'making it up'. And we *can* test them. We can read the Gospels. We can come into contact through the New Testament records with what, or rather whom, they asserted they had heard and seen. And when we do, does it look as if someone has 'made Jesus up'? Can we really believe that Christ is someone's invention? If so he must, or they must have been most remarkable, even greater than Christ himself, for the creator must be superior to his creation.

2. *The essence of the proclamation*

The strong point, therefore, in the Christian proclamation is Jesus—his life, his death, his resurrection. If we let this go, and there is no reason why we should, we have knocked away our own foundation. For this is certain, the Christian Gospel, the Church's message, the Apostolic declaration—call it what you will—rests on an historical event. Jesus come in the flesh. If we deny this, we have nothing distinctive to say.

And this is what John was contending for in his letter. During his time some people were beginning to assert that it didn't really matter if belief in Jesus of Nazareth as an historical person was firmly held. There could be belief in the Christ spirit discernible in human behaviour, and this would suffice. But John was adamant. The Christ spirit among us there must certainly be, but not at the expense of discounting the fact of Jesus, man of Galilee, Judaea and Jerusalem, who lived, died and rose again. Everything about Christianity is rooted in a datable historical event.

3. The ground of the fellowship

What is more, if this historical basis is destroyed, the Christian fellowship is broken. Note again what John wrote. 'That which we have seen and heard declare we unto you, *'that ye may have fellowship with us.'* He could scarcely express it more plainly. If the basic belief is destroyed the basic fellowship is destroyed. The fellowship of the Christian Church is rooted in belief in the man Jesus come in the flesh whom we call Lord.

APPLICATION

Today at the Lord's table we are seeking to express our fellowship. We do it by breaking bread and pouring out wine in remembrance of what Jesus did the night before his death. This is a spiritual service and the exercise is a spiritual one, but we shall lose all if we do not hold to the historical root. Jesus seen and heard.

SAINT JOHN THE EVANGELIST'S DAY

The man by the manger

> St. John 21.24 *'This is the disciple which testifieth of these things.'*

1. John the witness

In Greek the word 'testifieth' (μαρτυρῶν) has as its root the word 'martyr'. The Prayer Book will not let us get away from 'life losing' in connection with Jesus. Yesterday Stephen being stoned, tomorrow the 'Innocents' being slaughtered, today John testifying or 'martyring'. John was called to carry out his witness first by writing a book. Stephen was called to carry out his witness by his confession unto death. The Innocents were called to bear witness to a complexity of human existence, in which pain is innocently suffered, and in which God is involved.

2. John the Evangelist

We must notice that today is dedicated to John *the Evangelist*. There are many other appellations that could be made. John the Apostle, John the son of Zebedee, or even John the Martyr. What, however, he is actually called is John the Evangelist. That is possible because of the baby in the manger. It is because of him 'glad tidings of good things' were able to be brought. An evangelist can, therefore, exist, and an evangel come into being. Thus Saint John the Evangelist's Day *interprets* Christmas. It says Christmas has a produced a Gospel.

3. John the testifier

But this is not all. The lection from St. John chapter twenty-one is arresting because of the *content* of the testimony it gives to Jesus. It constitutes another set of answers concerning the identity of the baby in the manger. Who is he?

(1) He is one who knows our individual destinies. Peter asks, 'Lord, and what shall this man do?' The implication is, 'You know, Lord, you know all about each one.'

(2) He is the one who, like a King, does not divulge all his knowledge to his subjects, he holds the secrets of government. 'If I will that he tarry till I come, what is that to thee?'

(3) He is one about whom we must make individual and personal decisions, no matter what course others may pursue. The word to Peter is, 'Never mind about John, follow *thou* me.'

4. John at the door of the manger

To rise higher than mere sentiment at the sight of a baby calls for application of the mind. Do not, however, despise the sentiment. God stooped to a point as low as this so that we may *start* on the Christian way. *Where* we start is not important. The heights to which we advance are more important. John wrote his book so that by his testimony we might see the *significance* of the baby in the manger, and come to follow him. That is what the Evangelist says. We must listen to him. Especially must we listen at Christmas. Christmas without the Evangelist soon has little meaning. That is why the Prayer Book posts John the Evangelist by the manger. You may go in to the manger to see the Christ Child by yourself, but on the way out you will be stopped by the Evangelist. He will ask you what you have seen. And if you do not know, he will tell you. We are all advised to listen.

THE INNOCENTS' DAY

In praise of innocence

Revelation 14.5 (NEB) '*No lie was found in their lips.*'

1. *A man is a whole*
It has been said of the Greeks that they were more interested in the truth than in telling the truth. It may, however, be doubted whether a man can be so neatly parcelled out. A man is an inter-acting whole. If there is a perpetual lie on his lips there must be a perpetual lie in his soul. It is one of the sophisticated assumptions of the twentieth century that a man's tongue is not important. What he says in public matters little so long as he safeguards what he believes in private. But the two interact. What he says in public will *affect* what he believes in private. A perpetual lie on the lips must mean in the end a lie in the soul.

2. *Innocent lips*
This truth also works the opposite way. A man blossoms through his mouth. In other words the quality of his soul will

reveal itself in the words he uses on his lips. Innocence, there-fore, in the soul will be experienced as innocence in the lips. This phrase 'innocence in the lips' is worth thinking about. Words can be used to beguile people, to cheat them and to lead them astray. Such action should never characterize the Christian. He should possess innocent lips. Of Talleyrand it was stated that he used words, not to reveal his thoughts, but to conceal them. His lips were not innocent, nor was his intention.

3. *Innocence is perceptive*

Innocence may be counted childish. It is certainly the character-istics of a child. Plato, however, taught us long ago that loss of innocence does not qualify us for greater understanding. We often think it does. André Gide thought the Prodigal Son had to journey into the far country in order to grow up. But is the eye doctor a better doctor for having a disease in his own eyes? Does it make for clearer seeing? This is what Plato asked. And we could turn the question this way. Does a man stand a better chance of understanding truth by being a sinner? What Innocents' Day stands to tell us is that innocence sees further into goodness than does cleverness or even experience. We find this hard to believe, but it is what the New Testament cries out to tell us by hinting that the one who knew God to the closest degree was sinless and born of a pure Virgin.

'No lie was found in their lips.' No higher praise can be given. Innocent lips mean an innocent life. Such people live with God. It is the picture we are given in today's Epistle, the guileless before the throne of God.

4. *Our need of cleansing*

As then we seek God's sacramental presence we need to pray for cleansing, cleansing of the lips, cleansing of our thoughts. It is no wonder the Holy Communion service begins as it does, 'Almighty God, unto whom all hearts be open, all desires known, and from whom no secrets are hid; cleanse the thoughts of our hearts. . . . .' It is purity, it is innocence, innocence regained through the confession and absolution that leads us into the joyful presence of our Lord.

THE INNOCENTS' DAY

Jeremy and Jesus

> St. Matthew 2.17 '*Then was fulfilled that which was spoken by Jeremy the prophet.*'

I read on one of my Christmas cards,

> And therefore be merry, set sorrow aside,
> Christ Jesus our Saviour was born on this tide.'

Quite right. I did that. We all tried to do that. We set sorrow aside. But on the third day out from the manger we meet Jeremy, or Jeremiah, as we more commonly call him, the prophet of sorrow. The Prayer Book catches us by the arm as we are leaving the manger and says, 'Before you go, listen to Jeremy.'

1. *The tears at Christmas*

But Jeremy hurts. Tears hurt. Lamentation and great mourning more so. But when Jesus was born, *because* Jesus was born, that is what took place. Jeremy, who saw more clearly into human nature through his own sensitivity than most men, said it would be like that, and it was. At least, that is what St. Matthew records. Herod ordered the slaughter of 'all the children that were in Bethlehem and in all the coasts thereof, from two years old and under'. So he sought to secure an early death of Jesus. This is how there were tears at Jesus' birth as well as smiles, joy and sorrow intermingled, intermingled in connection with Jesus. And the question is, why? Two answers may be given.

(a) *Because Jesus is a divisive person*

The wise men rejoice over the child. Herod is wroth. It is the same child. But there are two effects, two contrary effects.

31

Jesus is a divisive figure. Later in the Gospel St. Matthew records the words of Jesus himself. 'Think not that I am come to send peace on earth. I came not to send peace, but a sword. For I am come to set a man at variance against his father, and the daughter against her mother. . . .'

(b) *Because Jesus is involved in an involved world*

The doing of good often produces an unwanted and unsought backwash of evil. Jesus became incarnate in that sort of world, the sort of world where because wise men worshipped, mothers were bereaved in Bethlehem, the sort of world where there is little joy without sorrow, little light without darkness, little healing apart from pain. And the mystery of the *birth* of Jesus is the same mystery as lies hidden in the *death* of Jesus, the mystery of vicarious suffering, mysterious not least because the vicarious sufferer is often *un*aware of what is happening. So it was with the Innocents. So doubtless with their mothers. Jeremy said life is like that, and St. Matthew says his words were fulfilled in Bethlehem. 'In Rama there was a voice heard, lamentations and weeping and mourning. . . .'

2. *Redemption involves suffering*

None of this is the children's side of Christmas. A man has to be an adult man, a woman an adult woman before either can begin to enter into the things that Jeremy says. Perhaps Jon Silkin had the kind of experience which qualifies, if we may judge from his poem, *Death of a Son* (who died in a mental hospital, aged one).

> Something has ceased to come along with me,
> Something like a person: something very like one.
> And there was no nobility in it,
> Or anything like that.
>
> He turned over on his side with this one year
> Red as a wound.
> He turned over as if he could be sorry for this,
> And out of his eyes two great tears rolled,
> like stones, and he died.

Not many Christians keep 'The Innocents' Day', perhaps not many can. Jeremy is not everyone's prophet. But he goes down deep, very deep, yet not too deep. Jesus is only a saviour if he is incarnate in our complicated world, being involved in its complications. There cannot be redemption without suffering. There cannot be a saviour apart from tears. We cannot help another in any profound way apart from pain. Pain is not always the sufferer's fault. It wasn't the Innocents' fault. Can we find our foothold here? Only just, I think, no more than 'only just'.

THE CIRCUMCISION CHRIST

The mark

It has been said that you can always 'spot' a sailor by the way he walks. It can be quite an amusing occupation when you are sitting in a bus or on a platform waiting, trying to guess what jobs you think people do, especially if you have a companion. It is a game which sharpens your powers of observation and your intelligence. The police, of course, make a serious business of this.

1. *Have Christians a distinguishing mark?*

Now let me ask my question. Is it possible to spot a Christian? Some people would say yes, just look for someone miserable. Perhaps you've heard of the host who was to 'put up' a clergyman for the weekend, a visiting preacher whom he had never met. He went to the station to await his arrival. But of all the men he saw swarming off the train and through the platform barrier, none wore clerical dress. How *could* he spot his guest? Last of all, in desperation he accosted what he thought was a likely person and enquired, 'Excuse me, are you the clergyman who is going to preach at our Church this weekend? The surprised man was dumbfounded. He couldn't think what to reply. Last of all he blurted out, 'No, no, not me, and I am so sorry I look like I do, but you see, I'm suffering from indigestion.'

Christians don't always look miserable, and it is only people who want to have 'a dig' at them say they do. But have Christians a distinguishing mark?

2. *The Jews had a distinguishing mark*

The people of God in the Old Testament certainly had a distinguishing mark. The Jews still have it today. And Jesus had it, and St. Paul, and no doubt all the Apostles. Let me tell you one or two things about it.

(*a*) It was a mark that could never in any way, except by serious mutilation, be eradicated. *It was life-long.* The Jew received it on his eighth day, and he carried it to his grave. It was absolutely and permanently indelible. It could never rub off.

(*b*) It was, however, in almost every instance the indication of *pure privilege*, that is to say, it was not earned. It was not the badge of personal merit. It did not indicate morality or any kind of religious awareness. It was given on the eighth day. It indicated parentage. It indicated racial blood.

(*c*) *It was divisive.* It was for men. Women were left out. The mark chosen could scarcely be more indelible and more exclusive of all and every female.

3. *The Jewish mark rejected*

There was a time when the early Christians thought that this mark, circumcision, ought to be compulsory in the Church. But Paul was against it. It was carnal, he said, it ministered to pride. The real mark of a Christian, he taught, was faith in Christ, faith which brought about a new creation. A hard struggle was fought but St. Paul prevailed. Circumcision was not made the mark of a Christian. Jewishness, nationality and race have no authority in the Church by any kind of right. That Jesus was circumcised *and* (note the 'and'), that no Christian must be circumcised in order to be a Christian could not cry out more plainly than it does the anti-exclusiveness and the spiritual basis of the Christian Gospel.

4. *Faith and Baptism*

But because the Jewish badge is not essential for Christians, we must not assert that no badge is necessary. Christians have a mark, but unlike circumcision it is personal, open to all and completely spiritual. It is faith in Jesus as Lord, borne witness to by baptism.

APPLICATION

Can you spot people who possess this mark, that is, those who exercise such faith? I think so. You do not have to be with them very long before you discover it. It governs their whole demeanour, their whole attitude to life and to other people. Has this congregation that clear, decisive Christian mark?

THE CIRCUMCISION OF CHRIST

Poetry and prose

Luke 2.15, 21 (NEB) '*After the angels had left them . . . the time came to circumcise him.*'

How dull! O yes, there would be a party, but how prosaic after the vision of the angels glorifying and praising God. There is nothing poetic about a circumcision; instead, tears, blood and a formal, not very attractive ceremony.

1. *The absence of poetry*

It is difficult for us to think of Christ at the centre of this occasion, but most important that we try to do so. The life of our Lord was not passed continuously in the realm of the poetic. The possession of strong spiritual life does not result in a life lived among lilies and vestments. There has to be prose as well, the long stretches of hard discipline where the dominant urge is duty. The angels are not always visible. We might gather from the Bible that they are rarely visible. We must not, however, reckon that in those days bereft of any poetry our spiritual vitality is less. The angels left Jesus, and he was the centre of a formal circumcising party.

2. *The function of prose*

The Word of God for us today could be one of encouragement to persist with our religious practices at those times, and they can be many, when they seem to be prosaic and no thrill or excitement is present, nothing remotely like the presence of an angel, or the poetry such represents. But we must not give up. Discipline as well as excitement is needed to give us character and capacity for mission. Jesus was not released from a formal religious exercise. What grounds have we for despising the value of such for our own development?

THE EPIPHANY

The outsiders

Ephesians 3.1 '. . . . *the prisoner of Jesus Christ for you Gentiles.*'

We only have to change one word here for the text to become alive. It is the word Gentiles. But read instead 'outsiders', because that is precisely what other races were as far as the Jews were concerned, *outsiders*. And here is St. Paul saying that it was in the cause of these outsiders that he became the prisoner of Jesus Christ. It was for preaching Christ to them that he found himself in gaol.

1. *Who are the outsiders?*

What does the word 'outsiders' conjure up in the minds of us who have come to a celebration of the Holy Communion? Does it suggest people who are not confirmed? People who never attend a church at all? People who profess no kind of religious awareness? People who do not think in terms of God's existence at all? People who glory in permissiveness? People who are tatty, aggressive and disturbers of the peace? Alcoholics? Drug addicts? Meths. drinkers? Who are the outsiders? Whoever they are, it was for people like this, and as varied as this (and there was no lack of vulgarity and crudity in the cities of the Roman Empire), that Paul was willing to suffer imprisonment.

2. *A fresh look at Epiphany*

We have to be careful about Epiphany. To paint pretty pictures of gorgeously robed kings arriving at some Renaissance styled manger to present their gifts is too easy and too unreal. The manifestation of Christ to the Gentiles is not like this. It is more likely to involve dinginess, the dinginess of a prison cell, the dinginess of some coffee bar, basement or derelict bombsite, half-lit rooms where drugs are pushed and bodies degraded. They are true followers of St. Paul who find themselves in such a world for the express purpose of somehow winning people from among them for Jesus Christ. Some *are* won.

3. *Two dangers at the Parish Communion*

It is easy for us who gather at the Parish Communion to look with superiority at those who never attend. The terror of the word 'outsiders' or the old word 'Gentiles' is that it can produce a special brand of spiritual snobbery. The peril of Judaism was Pharisaism. We have to be careful about this.

It is also easy for us to be satisfied that we are nurturing our own souls at the Lord's table, and this is all that matters. Epiphany stands, however, to cry aloud its reminder that our concern must also be with those who are absent. We have to strive and struggle for them, a costly and painful process. St. Paul was willing to be a prisoner, so much did he care about the outsiders. Is this the practical interpretation we put on the Epiphany? It ought to be.

THE EPIPHANY

By the light of a star

> St. Matthew 2.10 and 11 *'When they saw the star, they rejoiced with exceeding great joy. And when they were come into the house, they saw the young child with Mary his mother, and fell down, and worshipped him: and when they had opened their treasures, they presented unto him gifts; gold, and frankincense, and myrrh.'*

We have to take a firm grip on ourselves over this story. Unless we do, we are unlikely to get past the memory of some childish representation of the account. We shall see something like what Rex Knowles wrote about in *Guide-posts* in December 1961. His own children dragged him out from the sitting-room to see a play. The stage 'set' consisted of a lit torch wrapped in 'swaddling clothes' lying in a shoe box. There was Rex (aged six), wearing Daddy's bathrobe and carrying a mop handle. He was followed by Nancy (aged ten), announcing 'I am Mary and Joseph.' Next came Trudy (aged four), with flapping pillow cases over her arms, lisping 'I am an angel,' and finally Anne, (aged eight), riding a camel, at least she moved *as if* she were riding a camel, because she was wearing her mother's high-heeled shoes. She bowed three times before the 'Holy Family' and announced 'I am all three Wise Men. I have precious gifts, Gold, Circumstance and Mud.' That was all. The play was over. . . . And if you have ever spent Christmas with children, or if you were in my job, you would have seen many versions of the Wise Men story, most of them comic, though not meant to be.

But let's suppose we can get beyond our memories of childish representations of this story. Let us leave behind the literalists and come back for them another day. Let us ask ourselves what this piece of poetic representation of truth is saying to us.

1. Stars

It says first that the wise men were guided by *a star* to Christ. I expect this is true of us all, and we are wise if we let the thing happen. I mean, there was some intermediary which led us to Christ, it was not first the Christ himself that we saw.

My mind goes back a long time now to when I was a boy, and how I was attracted to the place of Christian discipleship, not by that life of faith which I didn't really understand, but because the Vicar at the local church had been an International Rugger player. I was drawn by his manliness. He was my 'star'.

I prepared the sermon this week sitting in front of a copy of Utrillo's picture *Église de Seine*. It represents a church situated at the end of a narrow French street flanked by houses and a garden wall. That church, like every church, is meant to be a star to the neighbourhood. Perhaps not very attractive. Perhaps not very bright. Nevertheless, a star guiding the residents of the district to Christ himself.

And we Church people ought to be stars, we ought to be men and women who, by the brightness of disposition, lead others to the ultimate source of all the world's brightness. It is not books nor philosophies, nor even sermons, that will lead people who are far outside the Church in the direction of a spiritual interpretation of life. It is the woman at Number Seven, the flat at the very top of that rather old-fashioned block where there is no lift, who greets everyone with a smile. It is the Managing Director who is scrupulously fair, but with cheerfulness, whom men observe. These people shine like stars in our modern overcast world. And they do not abound. Therefore they are noticed. Wise men even from afar will follow them and some even arrive at the source of light.

2. Gifts

We notice in the second place that when these wise men arrived at Christ's presence they presented gifts. There isn't much reality about a man's religion unless *he gives something*. The reason for this is that our gifts represent part of ourselves. That is why the taking up of a collection in the service of worship is part of the worship. The money doesn't go straight into the vestry and into the safe and tomorrow morning into the bank. It is taken to the altar and dedicated. Because every coin there on the alms-dish represents a person. It came out of someone's pocket or handbag. It was theirs. And they gave it willingly. If you want it in theological language, our gifts represent our self-oblation to God. These wise men when they arrived at Christ's cradle, worshipped *and then* they opened their treasures. The worship and the giving belong together. Indeed, if you examine the story carefully you will see what a remarkable penetration into spiritual experience the whole catena of events represents. There are five steps:

(*a*) They saw a star and followed it.
(*b*) They were puzzled and sought to make enquiries.
(*c*) They saw Christ.
(*d*) They worshipped Christ.
(*e*) They offered gifts to Christ.

3. *The way to benefit.*

The third observation I should like to make is about the gifts themselves. They are unusual—gold, frankincense and myrrh. Perhaps we might say that they represent wealth, culture and sadness. But they were all offered to Christ. That they were so offered shows that they are ineffective without the offering. Of course, we need some convincing of this. The world always has needed a good deal of convincing that gold itself is not the miracle worker. But wealth doesn't automatically produce happiness. Anyone in this church this morning over twenty must remember the glowing promises that were made, that if only poverty were done away with in Britain, and slums wiped out, and insurances provided, indeed the Beveridge Plan, then crime and violence and hooliganism would be gradually done away, because there would be no need. It is poverty that makes for crime. Is it? I hear just the opposite today. It is riches that make for crime. The hooligans have *too much* money. What *is* the truth? Isn't it that riches alone are insufficient? They must be dedicated to a higher purpose. Riches without worship are dangerous. The wise man presented his gold to Christ. Then his wealth was a benefit. It is a lesson crying out to be learnt in these our modern times.

And what about the frankincense? What about the culture? Dr. Leonard Griffiths, formerly minister of the City Temple, to whom I am indebted for some points in this sermon, likens it to science. Science is the modern enricher of life. We need to remember, however, that science, like wealth, cannot of itself solve the human problem. Our final praise must be for God. Perhaps the call for this is one of the most striking facts about this new genius France has produced, Jean Frêne. He is of peasant origin, but when they drafted him into the army, in an intelligence test where officers normally score eleven or twelve points, Jean scored seventeen and then nineteen. The government immediately sponsored his education and in six months he completed a course which takes a normal able student six years. At the centre for Nuclear Research in Lyons one professor describes Jean's mind as the most remarkable he has ever encountered and predicts that we may yet see another Einstein. Jean, however, is very modest and this is what he says, 'I know that only God is perfect, and therefore all praise and glory are his. Many French philosophers have said this, but I don't think it can be said too often. Man, no matter what he achieves, is always imperfect and in need of help. . . .' Is Jean Frêne following the wise men who presented their frankincense, symbol of culture, to Christ? It could be so. It could also be a lesson for us.

Thirdly, the wise men presented myrrh. This, too, is intriguing. It is so easy naïvely to expect that troubles are automatic educaters. They are no such thing. Man is at best only very slow to learn from past errors, and when he does, it is probably because he has taken his calamities to the feet of Christ and learned a better way.

APPLICATION

So Epiphany has come again to urge us to follow those stars that lead us to Christ. Whether we are rich men, cultured men or sorrowful men, or all three, our possessions will not profit us unless they are laid at Christ's feet. In practice this means being a man who worships, worships intelligently, worships consistently, worships with his fellow-men. Will you be that throughout the coming year?

THE CONVERSION OF SAINT PAUL

Your time, my time

> Acts 9.10 *'The Lord said to him in a vision, "Ananias."*
> *And he said, "Behold, I am here, Lord." '*

INTRODUCTION

Day after day the sun rose in an azure sky and shone magnificently till it had set. So it was in Britain in the early summer of 1940. But the country was 'at sixes and sevens'. Everything seemed to be going awry with the war effort. The House of Commons in particular was exasperated. For one man, however, this was his time. In a sense it was the time of his life. It was his καιρός as the Greeks would have said, his opportunity, the moment for which all his life was a preparation and upon which all in future would turn. This was Winston Churchill, for years cold-shouldered, disregarded and out of office, now invited to become Prime Minister. And he rose to his time. He rose to the occasion.

January 25th brings to our notice a man who rose to his time in connection with the conversion of St. Paul. It was Ananias.

Indeed, this is all we know about him, that he rose to his time, but humanly speaking, the overall development of Christian history is due to the fact that he, Ananias, did just that. His story is a highlighting of the importance of rising to our time. Let me tell you what that story is.

All Damascus was on edge. The Jews jubilant. The Christians cowering. News had filtered through that Saul the arch-persecutor was on the road. Soon he with his satellites would be smoking out the traitors to Jewry who looked to Jesus the carpenter Messiah. There would follow the knock on the door. the tearing apart of families, the filthy prison, the exile or the pit for stoning. Pity the Christians, now that Saul was on the road.

Then the rumour spread that Saul had been blinded. Then the more fantastic rumour that Saul had been converted. Then the fear in Damascus doubling back on itself that this was a trap to lure the Christians off their guard. And then a vision to one Christian. 'Ananias!' And he said, 'Behold I am here, Lord'. It was the time for Ananias. He knew it when the command followed. 'Go to Straight Street and ask for Saul. Behold, he is at prayer.'

What would you have done? What would I have done? No doubt at first exactly what Ananias did—protest! 'The thing is impossible. This man has done untold harm among Christians in Jerusalem and has now come to Damascus for the same purpose.' But the command was insistent. 'Go to Straight Street. Go to Straight Street. Go to Saul. He is not persecuting, he is praying. Saul is a key man. Through him the Gospel will be presented to whole nations and kings and even Israel itself. Go to Straight Street, Ananias. It is your time.' What would you have done? What would I have done?

There are at least three requirements when we know our time has come and the first is courage.

1. Courage

Think of Ananias, every step bringing him closer to Saul's lodging where he would have to knock and make enquiry.

Could he be sure it wasn't a trap? Perhaps Ananias was the leader of the Christian community in Damascus. Could he be sure this was not a device to pick off the head of the movement with the result that it break down? Could Ananias be sure that as soon as he knocked handcuffs would not be clapped upon his wrists? But Ananias continued along Straight Street. He knocked on the door. The door opened and he saw inside. . . . Ananias rose to his time but it called for courage.

2. Obedience

Secondly, a man's time calls for obedience. I think I know the only way Ananias got one foot in front of the other on Straight Street to go to Saul's lodging. It was because he heard a voice behind him commanding, 'Go to Saul, Ananias. Go to Saul.' It was fear of disobeying that voice that kept him on the road. There were few people Ananias could trust in Damascus just then. If he failed the commanding voice then, to whom could he run? But here was a word of encouragement. There often is with God's commands. 'Behold, Saul is praying. This is what you will see when the door opens. The persecutor praying.' Persecutors don't pray unless something stupendous has taken place. So Ananias went.

3. Lack of hostility

When a man rises to his time he must not be hostile to the forces that hitherto have hedged him in. And so we see Ananias stepping in from the bright sunlight in Straight Street to the darkened room where the blinded Saul was praying. We see him approach and lay his hand on Saul with words the like of which none more remarkable have ever been spoken. 'Brother Saul!' What a victory in Ananias' spirit. 'Brother Saul. God has sent me that you may recover your sight.'

APPLICATION

Has your time come? What if it comes tomorrow! What if it comes on your way home from Church today? What if

the call rings insistently in your mind? Go and visit that neighbour who is wretched and miserable. Suppose you are asked to
undertake a job that is most demanding? Have you the courage?
Will you obey? Will you be hostile?. . . . We ought surely to
pray at this Holy Communion service on the day of the
Conversion of St. Paul for grace to rise to our time, whatever
it is, that the whole Church will rise to its time, and that
opportunities are not lost through procrastination which is a
deadly enemy.

THE CONVERSION OF SAINT PAUL

No nice calculations

St. Matthew 19.27 *'We have forsaken all, and followed thee:
what shall we have therefore?'*

INTRODUCTION

I don't know if St. Paul ever asked this question, but St.
Peter certainly asked it. He even appeared to ask it in the name
of all the Apostles. 'Behold, we have forsaken all . . . what
shall we have therefore?' St. Paul forsook a great deal, perhaps
more than the twelve Apostles. 'What things were gain to me,
these have I counted loss for Christ.' There was his standing
in the legal profession. There was the purity of his personal
pedigree. There was his Roman citizenship. There was his moral
rectitude. All the assets which entitled him to belong to an
exclusive and upper society he lost when he became a disciple
of Christ. That is to say they did not count any more, even
if they continued to exist. They certainly constituted no
grounds for his standing with God. This depended solely on
the grace of God in Christ who appeared to him on the
Damascus Road saying 'I am Jesus whom thou persecutest.'

45

1. There are rewards for Christian discipleship

But is following Christ all loss? Is there no reward for the renunciations Christians make in the name of Christ? Is our Lord so hard a taskmaster? There are rewards; Jesus promised as much to the Apostles in answer to Peter's question. 'Anyone who has left brothers or sisters, father, mother, or children, land or houses for the sake of my name will be repaid many times over and gain eternal life.' Perhaps the greatest reward Christians gain is the secret of happiness. It is the very thing which eludes the world for all its grasping. Christians discover that as they grow less concerned with what they possess, so they are more and more conscious of what possesses them. Geoffrey Heawood in his book *The Humanist–Christian Frontier* has told us how there are some eight types of men and women who experience this and these are represented in what are called the Beatitudes at the opening of the Sermon on the Mount:

Those who are ready to do without; they have found the secret of living.

Those who accept the experience of sorrow, for they will find strength and courage grow in their lives.

Those who are prepared to be unrewarded and unrecognised, for the freedom of the earth is theirs.

Those who are passionately eager for what is fine and true and generous, for they will find these things.

Those who understand and make allowances for others, for they will find understanding of themselves.

Those who are utterly honest with themselves, for they will know God.

Those who create goodwill and reconciliation where they go, for they rank as God's sons.

Those who are ready to see things through in spite of any consequence: they have found the secret of life.

Yes, there are rewards for making the sacrifices of Christian discipleship, but they are connected with being rather than having, with spiritual things rather than material things. The rewards belong to a fresh scale of values, they belong to life of a different quality, what in fact is called in the New Testament 'eternal life'. That is what Christians gain.

2. We cannot calculate the rewards of Christian discipleship

It is no use, however, trying to work out precisely what the gains of discipleship will be. There may be nice calculations concerning capital gains in transactions on the Stock Exchange, but none in the spiritual realm. This is why Jesus said after promising the rewards 'But many that are first shall be last, and the last shall be first.' Those who have made apparently great sacrifices for Christ must not expect necessarily to gain great rewards. Those who made sacrifices of a humbler quality, or so it seemed, must not expect necessarily scanty rewards. We cannot calculate the things of the Spirit. We must simply do what Christ asks of us in our discipleship. Rewards there will be, but we cannot calculate or forecast them.

APPLICATION

Does all this cut Paul down to size? He seemed to make great sacrifices for Christ. The answer is, we do not know. The whole question of rewards and the future must be left in God's hands where it is safe. Our right course is to follow humbly.

THE PURIFICATION OF SAINT MARY THE VIRGIN

Dirty linen

Malachi 3.2 'For he is like . . . fullers' soap.'

1. Inevitable Soiling

Everyone has dirty linen. We may not like the fact, but it is true literally. Everyone at the end of the day discovers that however fresh was the undergarment in the morning, however crisp the nylon, however white the laundering had made it, by the evening it has become soiled. To live at all, to move about at all, to be active at all makes dirty linen inevitable.

This situation also holds in another sense. Personal relationships lose their freshness. Ideals become compromised. Standards of conduct are gradually lowered. It happens not only in individual experience, but in families, local communities, nations and international affairs. This is the dirty linen of life.

Do the Churches have dirty linen? Has organized religion all down the ages had dirty linen? Did the Temple in our Lord's day have it, and in the time of the Old Testament prophets? The answer is yes. All life in process of time becomes soiled, and this includes religious life. One of the chief purposes, therefore, of the Lord's coming to his Temple was to wash its dirty linen. This is what the portion of scripture appointed for the Epistle for today says, '... the Lord, whom ye seek, shall suddenly come to his temple; ....and who shall stand when he appeareth? for he is like.... fullers' soap.' Clearly the Lord's work is to cleanse his people, their life and their religion when it is soiled.

2. Cheating

The soiling of Israel's linen was due chiefly to cheating. We can deduce this from the list given in today's reading from Malachi. First sorcery, that is cheating in religion, a practice with a long history. Then adultery, that is cheating in the man-woman relationships of life. Next, false swearing, that is cheating in business. There follows cheating employees of their proper wages and cheating the fatherless and widows of their needs, and strangers, too, of their basic human rights. Finally, cheating God of the reverence due to him.

Is cheating the dirty linen of society at large? It is estimated that at present pilfering from shops costs Britain one million pounds a year. When the Lord comes to his people is his presence a judgement on their cheating? If so, it begins at the place of worship. Of Jesus it is recorded in the Gospels that when he entered the Temple in the course of his ministry it was first of all to clean it out, crying aloud that it had become a den of thieves, a place of cheating.

3. *Christ needed for wholesomeness*

What is the lesson of this scripture? It is to welcome Christ not only into our religious practice but into our public and private life as well. All the activities of man, even his religion, become soiled, cheating creeps in. Therefore we need 'the fullers' soap'. We need Christ as the purifier and refiner. We need him for our dirty linen.

4. *We must be honest to God*

At the present time there is a feeling that the Church's sincerity is soiled in the matter of what it professes in its creeds and formularies. Young people especially make this charge. They ask 'Are Churchmen really honest to God?' We must look at *this* linen. Maybe it needs washing. It would be surprising if it did not.

THE PURIFICATION OF SAINT MARY THE VIRGIN

About organized religion

> St. Luke 2.27 '... *the parents brought in the child Jesus, that they might do concerning him after the custom of the law.*'

This presentation of Christ as a child in the Jerusalem Temple restrains me. I have been less impatient with the inconsistencies of organized religion since I've understood the account. I have been less inclined to imagine that you can have a superior spirituality if you keep it apart from ecclesiasticism. I used to think so, but now I see that Christ was nurtured in customs of conservative religion, it is there that Christianity has its roots.

Perhaps you reckon this over sensitive. But you see Judaism *was* conservative. It was to some extent irrational. There was, for instance, a strong element of taboo in it. The Jews were self-conscious about the human body. They were shocked when the great Hellenistic movement swept down from Greece to

Palestine, and young men pursued their athletic exercises half naked in the gymnasiums. And for centuries childbirth had been regarded as unclean. The mother, after the birth of her baby was treated as unclean for seven days, and then she had to stay at home for a further thirty-three, until she could go forth to offer the specific rites of her purification.

1. Conservative religion

We find this irrationality disconcerting. It represents Victorianism plus. After all, we have now gone over to the other extreme, as witness the advertisements in every travel poster, magazine and advertising circular. So it it disconcerting to discover that it was within the confines of conservative organized religion that Christ was nourished.

I make this point lest in our modern liberal moods we too easily discard the old ways. I am a liberal. I find Judaism, unaired by Hellenism, too stuffy to be borne. But this I also observe, that if you plant your little seedlings out in the open garden too soon, they will quickly wither away in the sun or in the sudden wind. The tiny tender plant needs to be nurtured in a pot, a pot in a green-house, a pot which will constrict the plant when it grows too large, but a place of the limited growth it needs when it is young.

There is a place for religious conservation we do away with at our peril. We shall not nurture young plants, we shall not grow young Christians unless we have close guarded nurture, rules, regulations and restrictions. There are Christians like this, and organizations like this, and schools of thought like this. They are not for adults, not for adults in the faith, but you can't have gardens without greenhouses for the growing plants. You can't train up young people in homes and schools and other organizations without restrictions. Christ was nurtured amidst the restrictions of organized religion. It had its part to play, even in his training.

2. The liberalizing Christ

Secondly I should like to point out that when Joseph and

Mary brought in the child Jesus to the Temple to do concerning him after the custom of the law, he was recognized. He was recognized by Simeon, and he was recognized by Anna. We need not run to the conclusion that there was anything psychic about their perception of the identity of the child in Mary's arms. After all, the shepherds had talked in plenty about what they had seen in Bethlehem's cattle shed, only six miles distant from Jerusalem. The news would quickly reach the Temple ears. Daily the villagers trekked into the city bringing food to fill the market stalls. Simeon heard and Anna heard. But this is the arresting fact. They were not so confined by the orthodoxy of the setting that they could not recognize the Messiah. We are mistaken if we count orthodoxy something essentially restricted in its vision. What hinders spiritual perception is more likely to be worldliness than traditional piety. Men like a proportion of the priests in the Temple more concerned with political intrigue and 'rake-offs' in the Temple shop—*they* would not see the liberalizing Jesus coming to the Temple, as yet a tiny bundle borne in the arms of a girl about fifteen, but two orthodox worshippers saw him.

And Jesus *was* liberalizing. Simeon knew it. 'A light for revelation to the Gentiles,' he said, speaking this just *before* the line which follows, 'and the glory of thy people Israel.'

Yes, Jesus *was* liberalizing. See how he broke the stupid taboos of his day. He healed on the Sabbath, putting the priority of people before all institutions in a phrase which has rung down the centuries, 'The Sabbath was made for man, and not man for the Sabbath.' And he broke with the tradition of the Elders, all those constricting food regulations that have been a bondage to the Jewish people; and he talked openly with women, treating them as equals with men, to the astonishment even of his twelve Apostles. Jesus was a liberal, opening out religion to the fresh air and sunshine. But he never broke with the organized religion of his nurturing; to the day of his crucifixion he kept to its principles of ordered life and worship. He even kept the Passover the night before he died.

There are things wrong with the Church of England, as

51

doubtless with other Churches. The Leslie Paul Report much publicized in every daily newspaper is not without its telling truths. But we must be *careful* how we treat our organized religion. We must not so liberalize it till there is no place in it for children. We must not become so superior in our minds as to think that organized religion is no longer necessary. Reforms may be necessary. But reforms are not the Gospel. They will not convert England. Only men on fire with the love of Christ within our Church's life will touch our people's hearts. Do not despise organized religion. Do not neglect organized religion. Our Lord never did, but do not expect too much of it, even when it is reformed.

3. *Christ's willing condescension*

One more thought. *Mary* went through the rites of purification after the birth of Jesus. This is astonishing. I mean it is astonishing this fact has not been rubbed out of the Bible. After all, it stands there so awkwardly you would think that by now some Church authority embarrassed by this fact would have deleted it from the Gospel record. Christ has been counted as sinless, the Incarnate Son of God, the all righteous one. This has been the Church's faith. But here we see Mary treated as unclean after *his* birth. You would think the rite would have been suspended in his case. But no. He was treated just the same as every other child. Mary was treated just the same as every other mother. 'They did concerning him after the custom of the law.' No exception was made.

All of which suggests two things. One, that this record is true. Its awkwardness points to its truth. After all the motives for suppressing it stare you in the face. It is difficult, therefore, to resist the conclusion that what we have in chapter two of St. Luke is a Greek transcription of an Aramaic document, so primitive that subsequent theological conclusions had had no time to colour it. I say the account rings true.

And if it is true, it shows how close Christ came (and comes), to the conditions of our life. He stooped to the level of the ordinary, even to a personal acquaintanceship with irrational

52

taboos, and crabbed, conservative, confined religion. We can't, as his followers, be superior in our liberalism and rationalism after that. And we can't—and this is what I want to stress this morning, we can't reckon God has no room for us, humble, uninformed and elementary in our religious concept though we be. God comes to us as we are. He came to Jerusalem and he never deserted Jerusalem, even though it crucified him, the last of its prophets, outside the city walls. Christ takes people as and where they are, and never lets them go.

SAINT MATTHIAS'S DAY

Chosen at last

Acts 1.26 '. . . *and the lot fell upon Matthias; and he was numbered with the eleven apostles.*'

1. *A ministry lost*

Every now and then, not very often considering the number of clergy there are in the Church of England, but every now and then we pick up the newspaper to read of some vicar or curate who has made shipwreck of his ministry. Perhaps it is a case of embezzlement, robbing the parish funds, or some serious moral breakdown which leads to columns and columns in the newspapers, culminating in that terrible ceremony of unfrocking, as we call it, when a man who was *made* a clergyman in a cathedral, gets *un*made once again, perhaps in the same cathedral.

And you say, why remind us of this frightful possibility which does so much harm to the Christian cause when it becomes a reality? I do so because our Church bids me do so. It sets in the calendar February 24th, St. Matthias's Day, when we have to read how even an Apostle made shipwreck of his ministry, and had to be replaced by another whom the congregation chose. His name was St. Matthias.

I've had to chair some awkward meetings in my time, and so has every clergyman, and so have some of you who are not clergymen, but I wouldn't have wished to sit in Peter's place, chairing the meeting of which our Church has bidden us think in the closing days of February. He had to remind one hundred and twenty people in that upper room in Jerusalem, perhaps the same room where the Last Supper was celebrated, and from which Judas went out to betray their Lord, he had to tell them how Judas came to his sorry end, and hanged himself, a case of suicide, the suicide of an Apostle.

And there sat Peter in the chairman's chair, selecting a successor for Judas who betrayed his Lord, when he, the chairman, had that very same night denied his Lord. And it all had happened not eight weeks before, in that city of Jerusalem. How easily might Peter have been in Judas' shoes. There is not a world of difference between denying your Master and betraying your Master. And there was Peter sitting in the chairman's seat, and Judas' disembowelled broken body, a frightful castaway.

I can't think that Peter sat in the chairman's seat anyhow but humbly, and anyhow but gratefully. There, but for the grace of God might have gone Simon, son of Jonas, whom Jesus labelled Peter. And when you and I are tempted to despise the men who've made a shipwreck of their lives, we might think how easily, but for the grace of God, it might have been ourselves. Some little thing checked us. Some good fortune, perhaps long buried in the past, rose up to save us from perdition. None of us can reckon there is no danger lying anywhere in store for him. An Apostle chosen, called and trained by Christ fell to the place of a betrayer and then to death by his own hand. And Peter, too, was only saved by Christ's own prayers. Let St. Matthias' Day remind us of this solemn truth. 'Let him that thinketh he standeth take heed lest he fall. . . . '

2. *A ministry acquired*

And then the meeting set to choosing a successor to this Judas. Two names they set before the company, Joseph and Matthias, and fearing lest they chose entirely themselves, they prayed and then proceeded to casts lots, and the man who was selected was this man we call Matthias.

Now I do not know and cannot say, but there was a strength and weakness in the method of their choice. The fact is striking that we never read of anything Matthias did in all his ministry which followed, not even of his name. Was this the man designed of God to fill the empty place? Was the Church too keen perhaps, to fill the vacancy? May not St. Paul have been the candidate God had in mind? Was drawing lots the proper way to choose the Lord's Apostle? We do not know how right or wrong they were in doing what they did with Peter in the chairman's chair, but of Matthias there can be no doubt that he was true and faithful.

We are told that he had gone in and out among the followers of our Lord from the time when John baptized to the day of the ascension, and yet Christ never chose him out to be one of the twelve. Perhaps you've never been passed over in your life, and seen another nominated to a position you would have liked to occupy. If so, you cannot enter into St. Matthias's shoes. How did he feel when Peter was selected? How did he feel when Thomas was selected to be an Apostle? Thomas who doubted. How did he feel when Philip was selected? Philip, who was so very dull, and lacking in all enterprise. How did he feel when he saw Judas beckoned by our Lord to come and stand apart then with himself, a chosen man for Christ? And Matthias may have seen a trace of the fickleness of Judas' heart. But he, Matthias, was never chosen, his Master passed him over.

Have you ever been passed over for some task you would have wished to be selected for? How did you react? Did you sulk? Did you fret? Did you rebel? Did you cast in your hand and abandon the whole enterprise? If they wouldn't choose you they could do without you! Of Matthias we read that he continued with the Christian company although he wasn't chosen on the mount in Galilee to be one of the twelve. He continued faithful through the trial of Jesus, through the crucifixion of Jesus, through the resurrection of Jesus, through the days till the ascension of his Lord, and he was there in the upper room with Peter in the chair. Matthias, a holy and humble man of heart, of whom Paul would have been thinking when he wrote, 'Moreover, it is required in stewards that a man be found faithful.'

And when finally he was elected by a method which may have been right and may have been wrong, it could not have been easy to be known as the man who occupied the traitor's place. There are seats in the Church of England which have stories now attaching to them. I can think of a village in Norfolk. I can think of a Deanery elsewhere. It is not easy for the successors to those offices in the light of what has gone before. But Matthias would do it. Matthias would go through with it. Matthias had patience. Matthias was faithful. He knew no bitterness, he knew no resentment. He would continue to the end, a true and faithful steward of his Master.

3. *A word for us?*

Has this little-known Apostle's day, falling as it does close to Lent, any message for ourselves? Perhaps we reckon there is no need for us to pay attention to this season. We are strong, we are true, we need no special discipline. Then this is what this day asserts. 'Let him that thinketh he standeth take heed lest he fall.' An Apostle taught by Christ himself came to a sorry end. Better be like Matthias who came to occupy his seat, a patient man, a faithful man, a man who used what opportunities he had. And let us not lose this lesson as we pass it. Judas may be faithless, but God's work will go on ahead. He will simply choose another in the traitor's place.

In this church there will be a celebration of Holy Communion to mark the day of St. Matthias. I hope some will be there. But even more, I hope to see you during Lent at the services we hold, lest we lose our place, but rather keep our place, our Christian place, our place in Christ. We have to grasp it with both hands, it will not grasp itself. It is required in stewards that a man be found faithful, just like Matthias.

SAINT MATTHIAS'S DAY

The Christian agnostic

St. Matthew 11.25 '. . . *thou hast hid these things from the wise and prudent* . . .'

INTRODUCTION

I wonder what you would say is the greatest obstacle to Christian faith, or for that matter, the belief in God at all? The obstacles vary for different people. And sometimes they are trivial and trumped up. Like the woman who burst into the Vicar's vestry loudly asserting that she no longer believed in God, and when he enquired the reason, it had nothing to do with dissatisfaction over Cosmological or Ontological proofs (so called) for God's existence, even if she had ever heard of them, but because her boy had been turned out of the choir, and she wanted to get her own back on someone.

1. *The problem of pain*

It is the problem of pain that has seemed most contrary to the idea of a God of love. Yet if God's existence be denied on this account the explanation of life is not thereby solved. And suppose we shelve the question. Suppose we busy ourselves with our many mundane interests, sooner or later questions about the purpose of life and the finality of death push their obstructive heads into our secluded gardens. Some Christians have tried to extricate themselves from the problem of reconciling a God of love with the existence of pain by asserting that disease, perhaps even someone's particular illness, must be the will of God. In which case Sir Robert Platt is justified in asking 'How is it that it was God's will that children suffering from tubercular meningitis should die until about 1947, since when it is his will that they should live?' If, however, we improve on this, as undoubtedly we must, and recognize that disease is not due to the will of God, as Jesus'

E

action in curing it shows, and that it is often due to the ignorance and foolishness of man, this is still only half an answer. We could come back and ask why, if God is good, why doesn't he take active steps and eliminate the ignorance and foolishness of man? It is possible, of course, that he has taken such steps, and this is what the Gospel is about, but his action is neither automatic nor does it operate apart from the co-operation of man's free will.

2. Hard questions

These are hard questions, and we need to think long and deep, avoiding slick answers. Something, however, *can* be said by way of explanation, but only something. In the last resort we are left with mystery, just as we begin with mystery. And this is precisely the situation to which the Gospel for St. Matthias's Day draws our attention. There are things which God 'has hidden from the wise and prudent'. One particular hidden thing concerns Matthias. How is it that Jesus did not choose him from the outset to be one of the twelve Apostles? He was among the general company of the disciples from the earliest days of Jesus' ministry. How was it that Jesus chose Judas instead? Did he make a mistake? Did he not read Judas' character? Did he perhaps discern only too clearly what Judas' weakness was and hoped that appointment to a place of responsibility would overcome that weakness? Was Jesus wrong? And suppose he had passed over Judas and appointed Matthias from the start, would there never have been a traitor from among the twelve? Would Jesus have been betrayed at all? Would he then have been crucified? Then what becomes of the Gospel as we know it? These are hard questions and the answers are certainly hidden from human reason. Mystery remains.

3. Christian agnosticism

What course do we follow in this predicament? The answer is, we become Christian agnostics. Christians, be it noted. Not unbelievers, but believers who admit that there are many things we do *not* know, many questions we cannot answer. But because part of the sky is dark, the implication is not that there is no light at all. There is in fact sufficient light by which to walk, no more, perhaps, but at least that. And this we obtain not by a process of intellectual reasoning, though it has its part to play, but by faith. This is why the words of the Gospel proceed as follows: 'Come unto me, all ye that labour and are heavy laden, and I will give you rest.' Not knowing the answers to life's problems can be a burden. We shall not be completely relieved of it all our days. The path of man on this side of the grave will never be *flooded* with light. There is always the burden of not knowing. But if a man trusts Christ he will discover a way of living by which the burden is lighter. It may be that the man of faith seems a babe in comparison with the man of reason, but Jesus said 'I thank thee, O Father, Lord of heaven and earth, because thou hast hid these things from the wise and prudent, and hast revealed them unto babes.' The right course is to retain the child-like faith. The right course is to trust that Christ is the answer to the mystery of human existence. The right course is to use our reasoning powers as far as they will take us, on the basis of that faith; but the right course is also to be sufficiently humble to admit that there is much we do not know and perhaps cannot know. In this sense it is right to be Christian agnostics.

THE ANNUNCIATION OF THE
BLESSED VIRGIN MARY

Signs

How often we have heard the remark 'If only God would do something! If only he would show himself or give some sign of his presence!' We must not be scornful of this cry because quite often it is a real cry, a cry of anguish. There are people who really would like to believe in God, but the tragedies that overtake so many make faith difficult. To all such God seems to have hidden himself, to be doing nothing, and we are left alone with our tears.

1. *Signs already given*

But what can God do that he has not done already? He announced the birth of a son to a virgin. Surely this was a sign of God's presence! But how do we know those birth narratives in the Gospels are not legendary? Jesus performed miracles. But even if we take these as factual, might not some at least of the healings be capable of psychological explanations? There was of course the resurrection of Jesus himself; scholars, however, are not wanting who declare that what arose was the crushed faith of the Apostles in Jesus.

2. *The problem of signs*

This is the trouble with signs, in the absence of faith they can be explained away. Signs *require* faith, they do not produce faith. This is why Jesus was very hesitant to use his extraordinary powers. This was why he would not acquiese in the devil's temptation to throw himself down from the top-most pinnacle of the temple and walk away unhurt. And the reaction to Jesus' walking on the water could simply be—How does he do it? What is the trick? Signs and wonders do not necessarily evoke faith.

3. *An exceptional case*

There are exceptions. In the portion of scripture appointed for the Epistle for today, King Ahaz was bidden by Isaiah to ask for a sign. The situation with the enemy at the city gates was so desperate Isaiah risked the calling out of Ahaz's faith by means of a sign. 'Ask it either in the depth, or in the height above.' But Ahaz refused. He did not want to believe. And so a sign of a different kind was given. Before a young woman about to be a mother gave birth to her child, the land would be so overrun by the enemy that the only food available would be that of a wandering people, butter and honey. So they would experience the truth that God is with us (Immanuel), with us in judgement.

4. *The purpose of signs*

How shall we sum this up? Signs and wonders do not often produce faith in God, so do not lay great store by the miraculous. But for those who do believe, having made the leap of faith in the dark, signs of God's presence can be most encouraging. In the last chapter of St. Mark's Gospel there occurs this striking verse, 'these signs shall follow them that believe'. The phrase is worth noting. Signs that *follow* faith. And do not forget that after Mary, mother of Jesus had believed the message of the angel, then it was that he gave her a sign to reassure her. 'Behold, Elizabeth thy kinswoman, she also hath conceived a son in her old age.' It was not surprising that Mary ran to see for herself. This is what signs do, this is what they are for, to confirm the faith we already possess. It is in God's mercy that they are given. It is part of God's condescension to our frailty.

THE ANNUNCIATION OF THE BLESSED VIRGIN MARY

The vocation of woman

> St. Luke 1.38 *'And Mary said, "Behold the handmaid of Lord; be it unto me according to thy word."'*

At this service the subject for the preaching is really chosen for us, because today is 'Lady Day', the day of the Annunciation. It is 'The Vocation of Woman'. The day says, have you really applied your Christian faith to the position of woman in society?

Some men, of course, never take this seriously. The whole subject is a music-hall joke. Even worse, woman is taken as the instrument of man's satisfaction. But there is a proper Christian estimate of woman, and Lady Day could serve to remind us of it. I would even go so far as to say Europe is in urgent need of being reminded of it. Life is never healthy without a proper estimate of woman.

1. *Equality of status*

First of all we need to make the point that in the Christian understanding of men and women they are both of equal value. Women are not second-class beings. Whenever I conduct a marriage service I am always careful to point out that the words in which the man takes the woman, and the woman takes the man are identical, with one small exception, the word 'obey'. This tiny word safeguards the man's *ultimate* responsibility for his wife, but that being so, they take each other on *equal terms*. This equality of status is the gift the Christian Gospel has made to mankind. We do well to receive it and to encourage all those liberating movements which enable woman to rise to her equality of status and throw off the bondage of man.

2. *Differentiation of function*

We need to look in the second place, however, to see what this equality of status means. It means, roughly speaking, that 'women are as good as men'. What it does *not* mean is that they have the same functions as men.

Now the twentieth century urge on the part of some women to demonstrate that whatever men can do, women also can do, is of very limited value. Granted, women have proved their point. They have scaled mountains, swum the channel, flown aeroplanes solo, become barristers and judges, entered Parliament, achieved fame in the realm of science, and even engaged in heavy engineering. It is not easy to think of any sphere now where women have not shown that they can do what men do. They have proved their point. But where do we go from here? What is the next step? Do women now dress like men? Is the goal reached now that in some dens in Soho, so I read, you can only tell which is a girl by looking at her feet! Are women to behave like men? I am not answering the questions, I am only asking them. Is there now nothing more to be achieved in women's struggle than the aggravating problem about equal

62

pay for equal work? It is curious how in our modern way of looking at things, the end product is nearly always a question of money.

I believe that if woman's struggle for freedom has taken place so that she can be like a man, the struggle will prove to be not only useless but detrimental, detrimental to herself, detrimental to men and detrimental to society in general. Woman's struggle for freedom is only of value if it gives her freedom to develop her womanhood, to develop the thing which she has to offer to society, for lack of which it deteriorates. And what is that thing?

3. Woman's gift to society

This is the third point we need to make. *What woman has to offer society is the element of caring for people.*

If we try to make an assessment of what is going on in Western civilization at the moment, we cannot fail to note the progressive domination of the machine. This is a machine age. It will soon be the electronic age, but that is really only a sophisticated version of the machine age. Now it does not need a very subtle perception to observe that a machine age is a soulless age. Aldous Huxley has certainly pointed this out. And when machines get wedded to war, the outcome is disastrous. Nor can any of us fail to notice that machines are the special interest of men. If a car breaks down in the road, it is not the women that gather round it. In general terms life organized by men means machines, money and materialism. And that is twentieth century Europe.

This, then, is the context in which the vocation of woman is to be exercised. It is her calling in life to redress the balance of mechanization, materialism and soullessness. Which being the case, it should be fairly obvious that if woman thinks the end of her struggle is that she should become like a man, she has lost her way. What woman has to offer society is the element of caring for people. By all means let her have freedom, let her climb mountains if she wants to, stay down pot-holes and try her hand at chemistry; but if the aim is not to be a woman, she has failed, not only herself but the community in general.

Expressed in sharper and more pictorial terms, what Europe needs today is a mother. Time was, and not so long ago, when Mary, the mother of Christ, caught up and focused for a large part of Europe the longings of humanity for a mother. Society is unable to get along without a mother. It is said a child bears the mark all his life of having been brought up without either father or mother, but to be deprived of a mother is more harmful than to be deprived of a father. What is true of individuals is true of society as a whole. The nurture of the human race is not possible without the thing woman brings, caring for people.

But that is not all woman brings. She brings mystery, the non-logical, (I did not say illogical), and the intuitional approach to reality. Technological man scorns these things, but technological man will bring civilization to its death, and that very soon, unless the balance is redressed.

What is the vocation of woman? It is to bring soul into mechanized existence. Women are equal in status to men, but this does not mean they have the same functions as men, and if they think they have, they will be the losers and so will society. There are few things more absurd than rivalry between the sexes. In the purpose of God they are meant to be complementary. Together they provide what life requires.

APPLICATION

And someone is thinking, yes, all very interesting, no doubt, but what has this got to do with me? The answer could be, to accept ourselves for what we are, and not to try to be what we know we are not. This attitude of acceptance was the great characteristic of the woman we Christians revere most, Mary, mother of Jesus. She said 'Be it unto me according to thy word.' This is acceptance, perhaps the most fundamental practical principle in the whole art of living. Accepting ourselves. Being what we are. Not fancying we are geniuses (men). Not imagining we are prima donnas (women). Each man, each woman accepting the person, the gifts and the situation life has provided, and being ourselves. There is a place for each one of us, a task for each one of us, yes, and a final destiny for each one of us, too. Be what you are, a man, a woman in a new relation to God through Christ. This is the Gospel. This is the good news. This is the basic Christian proclamation. This is the kerugma.

ASH WEDNESDAY

Corporate guilt

Joel 2.12 ' "Turn ye even unto me" saith the Lord, "with all your heart, and with fasting, and with weeping, and with mourning." '

1. Brighter services
It is the last three phrases that stick, the phrases about fasting and weeping and mourning. We are not reluctant to turn unto the Lord with all our heart, providing the hymns are sung pretty fast, and some of them with a good beat, and modern rhythm; and if some drums can be included, at least for some, so much the better. We almost have a complex today about brightening up our services.

2. The danger of hypocrisy
And the fashion for 'jollying-up' isn't our only problem. You can't *make* people fast and weep and mourn. The result would be an appalling unreality. Imagine a congregation of strong young men and women trying to look miserable because Ash Wednesday orders this mood. It is impossible to put on attitudes just like a suit of clothes without being a hypocrite. And if anything is against the modern outlook, it is being insincere or appearing to be what you are not.

3. Where guilt is felt
Perhaps, however, we might do well to recommend some

humbling of ourselves for the *corporate* guilt of our times. Guilt over Vietnam, hunger and homelessness, is certainly not absent from the younger generation today. It feels most strongly and some are prepared to make sacrifices on behalf of these causes.

APPLICATION

Ash Wednesday, then, could be a day when we increase our sensitivity to the many blots upon our Western civilization, and a day to put into practice our determination to help relieve these necessaries by ways open to us. This could be our intention at the Holy Communion today.

ASH WEDNESDAY

Secret religion

> St. Matthew 6.16 '*But thou, when thou fastest, anoint thy head, and wash thy face. . . .*'

Lent is the time of self-denial, but the Gospel says we must not advertise our abstentions. For example, when we fast we must anoint our heads and wash our faces, so that men may *not* see that we are fasting. In other words, our religious exercises of this kind must be kept secret, no-one must know about them except God.

What do we learn from this?

(a) There is a *false form of Christian witness*. It is to draw attention to ourselves by our appearance. Some misguided Christian women imagine that they are witnessing to their Lord by the drabness of their clothing, and their deliberately outdated hair-style. Some men make a parade of all but complete absence of pleasure and leisure from their lives. All efforts at trying to be different from other people at any time, not only in Lent, as an end in itself is wrong. Real religion does not consist in being outwardly different from others, but rather in looking like other people, but being different inside.

(b) *Self-denial can be unrewarding.* This is when we exercise it for the sake of publicity. Perhaps it would be more accurate to say that it is *almost* unrewarding, for there *is* the satisfaction of being talked about, if that is a satisfaction. The Pharisees enjoyed it, anyway. Jesus said, 'They have their reward.' But it is all they get. No closer approximation to God. No growth in selflessness, no development of the kind of strength that endures in isolation. In order to be rewarding in these deep ways, no-one must know what our self-denials are, we must appear no different from those who make no special effort in Lent.

APPLICATION

Let us be quite clear. Jesus did not say, 'Do not fast'. There is no ground for a non-observance of Lent. He said, 'When thou fastest.' He took abstinence for granted on the part of a Christian. We must be ready for this first, but when we are, we must in the second place make sure that our abstinence is not showy, ostentatious, or concerned with externals. Otherwise ours will be a wasted Lent, when it could be a profitable Lent.

THURSDAY BEFORE EASTER

The proclamation

> 1 Corinthians 11.26 *'For as often as ye eat this bread, and drink this cup, ye do show the Lord's death till he come.'*

I wonder what you would say we are doing when we assemble, as now, this Maundy Thursday evening, at the Lord's Table? We might answer, keeping the anniversary of the institution of the Holy Communion by our Lord himself; or coming as individuals to strengthen our inmost souls in communion with

Christ; or demonstrating our togetherness as Christian people in the presence of him from whom the whole Church derives its existence and continuance. And none of these answers would be wrong. What, however, the text which I have selected from the Epistle says is that every act of communion with the broken bread and outpoured wine is a *proclamation*, a showing forth, almost an advertisement of the Cross of Christ. The word 'show forth' here is καταγγέλλω, and often used of preaching, as for example, St. Paul in Athens, 'what therefore ye worship in ignorance, this set I forth (καταγγέλλω) unto you.'

1. *The congregation's sermon*

So by our coming together we have made possible once again in act-form the showing forth of what happened on Good Friday, Christ's body broken on a cross and his blood outpoured. This is what God in Christ did 'for us men and for our salvation'. When we gather together to break the bread and receive the cup, that is what we are proclaiming. So this service is the *congregation's sermon*. In being here together, you and I are preaching Jesus Christ, and him crucified.

2. *The basis of all preaching*

I would ask you to notice that this action-sermon which we are preaching is regulative. That is to say, not only have we this Maundy Thursday evening gone *back* in mind to Christian origins, back to that upper room, back to the Lord sitting there with the Apostles, but we have gone *down*, down to basic principles, down to the basis of what all preaching, whether by action or by words should be, namely, a showing forth of Jesus Christ, and him crucified. We *need* this return to basic principles. Preaching can degenerate into moralizing, philosophizing, even into presenting programmes for political action and economic stability. No doubt these have their part to play, but unless preaching is rooted in what God did in Christ at Calvary, it is not Christian preaching, and sooner or later becomes irrelevant. Only the Cross has an abiding message.

Now it is not possible to celebrate the Holy Communion without breaking bread and without pouring out wine, but it *is* possible to preach with a complete disregard of what those signs show forth, that is why we say the Holy Communion is regulative. What we do here in this action-sermon is what should find a place in all preaching, a showing forth of Jesus Christ, and him crucified.

3. *Christ-centred Christianity*

Thirdly, you will notice that all the concentration here is on what God did for us. Today, and we are not all that different from the ages that are past, we concentrate on what *we* can do. What we can do for ourselves, what we can do for the under privileged, what we can do for society. We are in the centre of the picture. As far as God is concerned modern man has decided to 'go it alone'.

The Holy Communion does not ask us to do anything except to confess our sins, receive what he offers, and then thank him for the benefits. That is our Eucharist. Let us make no mistake, this is the point at which true religion begins and continues, in putting God's action for us at the centre, and ourselves as humble recipients on our knees at the circumference.

An article in the *Times Literary Supplement* of March 23rd, 1967, pointed out that the religious men who changed the politics of their day were men who spent much time on their knees. That is real religion. The so called religious men today who deliberately seek to advance good political causes spend much of their time in earnestly talking at Committees—and add very little enlightenment. They can even make matters worse as they did in the "twenties" puffing up the League of Nations, which turned out to be toothless.

It is men and women going out from God, from communion with him, on their knees, that make a difference in the world. A Christ-centred life is the only effective Christian life. I know about the dangers of pietism. I, too, have read what happened in nineteenth and early twentieth-century Germany. But for all our concern about contemporary conditions of existence, we must first and foremost and continually come to the centre, to which the Holy Communion calls us. Christ crucified for us. 'As often as ye eat this bread, and drink this cup, ye do show the Lord's death till he come.'

Let us therefore realize this evening the importance of what we are doing. We are proclaiming by our action what is central in all Christian discipleship. At the Lord's Table we are *at the centre*, at the heart, at the home of our faith. The right attitude is to be open to what the Lord has done, and will do for us still, even in this Sacrament.

THURSDAY BEFORE EASTER

Forgiveness

St. Luke 23.34 *'And Jesus said "Father, forgive them, for they know not what they do." '*

1. *The story*

Marcel Jouhandeau, a prolific twentieth-century French writer tells this story.

A young woman whose husband was a prisoner of war in Germany had three children on her hands and a small farm to maintain. This being the case, it was not surprising that she engaged a young man to help on the farm. but unfortunate that she picked on one of the worst, a splendid-looking young ruffian invalided out of the navy for cirrhosis of the liver, so swaggering he carried the nickname of the Cadi.

This scoundrel quickly gained ascendancy over the young wife who soon became his mistress. More than that, he so fascinated her there was nothing in her power she wouldn't do for him, even selling off part of the livestock, the furniture and the household linen to feed him sumptuously and to fill his pocket.

In 1944, towards the end of the war, her husband was released from prison. Two courses lay open to the Cadi, to stay on the farm or to go. For the wife there was only one course, so infatuated had she become, it was to keep the Cadi. That meant getting rid of her husband. So with the Cadi she made a plan. It would be executed in the milk-shed with a length of rope. But the device miscarried. What is more, the husband, Ducourtial, caught his wife as well as the Cadi, attempting to take his life; but the trick failed because her nerve failed.

At once both men left the young woman. The Cadi as fast as his legs could carry him to save his skin. The husband, to think things over. He had known the day he returned to his farm that he had lost his wife's love. He also knew that he had not lost his love for her. He had ordered the Cadi to go, but had not made a scene. Now even though she was implicated in trying to get rid of him, he loved her still. Next morning he returned to talk to her.

One glance told him how she had spent the night: in terror and anguish, expecting him to return with the police. But he brought no police. Instead he said, 'If you can manage to give up life with this man, I am willing to start with you again. If you cannot manage it, if my love and my forgiveness make no difference to you, then you can go with this man and I will seek no revenge. I will not trouble you. It is the children that count on your honour'.

At first she didn't reply. She was too stunned. Then she broke into sobs and rushed to clutch at him, but he eased her gently away. 'Whatever you do, do not embrace me', he said, 'it is all too near. Let the days slip by, and if I find your heart once more going with mine, we shall come closer bit by bit.'

'You're right', she said, 'but there are two things I want to say. Last night I saw what I had become, and I saw what you are, the best man in the world. You won't find me thankless. I shall never deserve the forgiveness you offer me.'

She kept her word. She never saw the Cadi again, except to make a final break. Within six months they were living together again as husband and wife, and the children were happy.

But the village couldn't take it. They couldn't take such an example of forgiveness in their midst. They couldnt't bear to see such a happy home within their community. They said Ducourtial's forgiveness was weakness. Not content with whispering, they insulted him to his face. Still he went on loving his Anna. Still he never lost an opportunity to defend her honour.

Then Anna fell ill. Ducourtial spared no expense, no trouble to obtain the service of the best physicians he could find. He never left her bedside during the six weeks that proved to be her last, not even though she was dying of some nameless disease that disfigured her beyond recognition. And when the coffin was carried along the street, Ducourtial followed, worn to a shadow.

One woman, Elise, always talkative, said 'At any rate, there's a true Christian.' But no-one was listening. They couldn't forgive this man and this woman in their midst who had *not* lived like everybody else. They couldn't forgive this couple for not being second rate. And so, because they couldn't forgive, they couldn't see the glory in their midst.

2. *The lesson*

If we do not accept the forgiveness we do not see the glory

The night before he died, Jesus took a cup and said 'This is my blood of the New Testament, which is shed for you and for many for the remisssion—for the forgiveness of sins.' Those words stand at the close of the consecration prayer which you will hear in a few minutes. And on the cross where Jesus shed his blood he prayed 'Father, forgive them, for they know not what they do', words we have already heard in the Gospel for today. Forgiveness costs. It costs terribly. It may cost blood. But it is in forgiving that we recognize the Christ in every Christian. What is more, it is in being willing to accept God's forgiveness that we become, and stay Christians. Forgiveness is at the heart of the Christian way, costly forgiveness. Not all will take it. But those who do see the glory in their midst, and only they.

SAINT MARK'S DAY

Our several callings

Ephesians 4.11 *'And he gave some to be Evangelists.'*

1. *Mark's background*

In his book *The Gates of the New Life* (T. and T. Clark, 1937), that moving Scottish preacher, James Stewart, has a striking sermon about St. Mark. It is called 'A drama in four acts'. First he gives us two facts about Mark: he was the cousin of Barnabas, that enterprising and lovable Christian man who featured so much in the first days of the young Christian Church; and secondly, he was brought up in a home in Jerusalem which played an important part in the development of that Church. So Mark had an excellent background, secure, stable and believing.

2. *The drama in Mark's life*

But Mark's life did not run smoothly, and this is why it has been presented as a drama in four acts. Barnabas brought his young cousin into the work on which he was so enthusiastically engaged. But experiencing the hardships, Mark ran away. He ran away from the mission. This was his *recantation*. We may suppose he retreated to the comfort of his home in Jerusalem. But when he thought, and when he heard, of the rigours Barnabas and Paul were facing and from which he ran away, *remorse* ate into his soul. So a third act in the drama of the young man came to be played out, it was his *restoration*, his restoration to the fellowship of Paul who no doubt despised this weak-kneed recantation. But he forgave Mark, and had him back, and Mark regained sufficient nerve to endure Paul's imprisonment as his servant. And then fourthly, Mark's *reparation*; he who had run away from the mission now contributed to the mission by writing that striking picture account of Jesus we call St. Mark's Gospel.

3. God's calling for each one

And now we call him 'Mark the Evangelist', Mark the mission-er. How strange that he should come to such a calling! But it was God's purpose that this should be.

> God moves in a mysterious way
> His wonders to perform.

Some are called to be Apostles and some prophets and some evangelists (that is what the Epistle for today affirms). And some Churchwardens and some organists and some choristers and some housewives and some school-teachers and some motor mechanics; we could prolong the list. This is what St. Mark's Day is crying aloud to tell us, that God is working his purpose out with each one of us. It is for us to accept what he ordains. This way comes peace of mind, accomplishment and inner satisfaction. We each have our several callings in and through God's providence.

SAINT MARK'S DAY

Pruning

> John 15.2 (NEB) 'Every fruiting branch he cleans . . .'

In the northern hemisphere the pruning is over by April 25th. The apple trees are finished in January or February at the latest and the roses by the end of March or early April.

1. The necessity of pruning

At one time I took on a garden in which there were thirty apple trees. That would seem sufficient to keep a supermarket in supply, but it didn't. Those trees had not been pruned for years. The branches were intertwined. Lichen had formed on them and there was any amount of dead wood. Worse still, because the pruning had been delayed so long, not even drastic use of the knife could restore the trees to health. Every fruiting

74

branch has to be pruned, it has to be cleaned. It is an operation the lazy man neglects, and so gets no fruit. It is drastic treatment the amateur is afraid to carry out and so he, too, gets no fruit. Fruit-bearing trees must be pruned.

2. *The necessity of discipline*

Nowadays the idea of discipline is unpopular. Certainly the notion that young people are better for the cutting experience of suffering is out of fashion. Some might even count this unwarranted harshness. But gardeners are not harsh men. They are usually kind, tolerant men. They know, however, that fruit trees not only have to be cut back, but vines have to be fastened to wires, perhaps attached to walls. The novelist Philip Gibbs has a story in one of his books of an older man peering into the face of a young violinist in Moscow, holding him at arm's length. He was pained, genuinely pained at the privations the young man was having to undergo because of the harshness of the Soviet system. 'However', he said, wagging his head, 'it will be good for your violin.' Very little artistic work of value is created apart from suffering. Very few great Christians are inexperienced in the meaning of pain. Fruit bearing requires the pruning knife. Character demands the sternest discipline and discipline always hurts.

3. *The necessity of incorporation*

If you travel around the orchards of Kent in January, as likely as not, you will see on the ground large piles of severed branches. They are left there to dry out, then they are collected and finally burnt. And if there is any disease on the branches their destruction is essential. But even if healthy and left on the ground in the orchard itself, no fruit will appear on them. This is obvious. The branches must be attached to the tree, that is to say, the pruned, the cleansed branches must be attached to the tree if fruit is to result.

Discipline of life is essential, but discipline is not enough. The Christian must be incorporated into Christ. He must be incorporated in the body of Christ. So will the life of Christ flow into him, making possible the fruits of Christian character, love, joy, peace, longsuffering, gentleness, goodness, faith, meekness, temperance. Mark underwent sharp suffering in his relations with Paul, he was for a time outside the fellowship of the Christian mission, but came to be reincorporated. This is how we have the Gospel according to St. Mark. It is the product of pain, discipline and reincorporation.

When we come to the Holy Communion, it is to be reincorporated into Christ, the Christ who himself suffered the pruning knife. Character comes through discipline. Life comes through attachment to Christ. Communion is vital.

SAINT PHILIP AND SAINT JAMES'S DAY

The rich man

James 1.11 *'So also shall the rich man fade away in his ways.'*

It was spring time in Rome and the bougainvillaea hung in delicate heliotrope tresses on the chrome walls of the ancient buildings. The Spanish steps were ablaze with the brilliant red of potted azaleas creating a richness in the evening sun beyond compare. Even the grass in the Borghese gardens was green; but it would not remain so, not in the heat of the Italian summer. 'For the sun is no sooner risen with a burning heat, but it withereth the grass.' This is so in all Mediterranean lands.

1. *What money can do*

And today's Epistle says the rich man fades away in similar fashion. We find this hard to believe. Well fed and expensively clothed, he appears to do everything but flag. He even shines in his luxury. But does he? Are rich men notoriously happy?

These people who have a 'lucky break on the pools', do they reply to those newspaper reporters who make enquires that life has suddenly become wonderful? Apparently not. It is asserted that the wealthy who spend their lives in pursuit of happiness exhibit a frightening boredom, especially (it seems), on luxury cruises in the Caribbean. What does this mean? It means that unless the rich man is careful, something withers *inside* him because of his riches. Then he becomes narrow, suspicious and absurdly unadventurous. Riches are not an evil, but unless they are handled courageously their effect can be disastrous. Jesus said 'How hardly shall a rich man enter the kingdom of God.' And remember the kingdom of God is not primarily some future state of bliss beyond the frontier post called death, first of all it is the reign of God's love in the heart *now*. Riches can be a killer as far as love is concerned, the experience of God's love and the expression of human love. Rich men must learn how to handle riches.

2. *Riches other than money*

The reaction to what the Epistle says about the rich man could be glee. (Sub-Christians and non-Christians like rich baiting.) Or the reaction could be boredom, thinking the words are of so limited an application (today's publicans, that is tax-gatherers, see to that), therefore we need not bother. But there are riches other than money. Some people are rich in the security of their married life; their home, their family and their relations stand all around them. These are family-centred people, do not expect largeness of heart there. And others have riches of the mind. Too easily these can produce intellectual snobbery, the destroyer of charity in the soul. Do not, therefore, count riches only in terms of pounds and dollars. All kinds of riches can cause the soul to shrivel. It is giving that leads to greatness, not possessing and certainly not hoarding.

3. *The source of freshness*

The first Psalm in our Psalter has a picture of a tree that does *not* wither. Unlike the grass burnt up with the burning heat of summer, its leaf stays green. And the reason is because its roots reach down to the water in the stream beside which it is planted. The roots of the life of the rich man, yes, and the not-so-rich man—must reach down through his riches if strength to stand fresh and attractive is to be experienced. And the stream consists of spiritual principles embodied in Jesus and made available in Christ who, though he was rich, became poor, that we, through his poverty might become rich. It is in communion with him that we learn the secret. Rich men can learn it too.

SAINT PHILIP AND SAINT JAMES'S DAY

One worry

> St. John 14.1 2 *'Let not your heart be troubled: ye believe in God, believe also in me. In my Father's house are many mansions: if it were not so, I would have told you. I go to prepare a place for you.'*

1. A place in heaven

Yes, it is comforting. No doubt Philip and James, together with the other Apostles were comforted when they reflected that there was a destiny in heaven for each one of them, a place where they would, each one, with his own peculiar idiosyncracies fit, just like a key in a lock. And it is true, but is it the correct meaning of this verse?

2. A lodging on the road

The word translated 'mansion' means 'abiding place', 'resting place'. The picture is of the Eastern dragoman going on before, to prepare his master's temporary lodging on the barren road ahead. There would be many such resting places prepared on an eastern journey, and they were all temporary.

3. Unreal worries

Jesus told his disciples they were not to worry, because he was their dragoman whom they should trust. We are not to worry:

(a) *at the variety of different religious expressions we see around us.* Fundamentalist, Orthodox, Catholic. Christ prepares many temporary resting places.

(b) *at the variety of forms even our religious experience may have taken.* There is no need to be ashamed at the various religious stopping places where we have been.

(c) *at the different forms of Christian message different preachers proclaim.* What they offer are only temporary resting places.

4. One real worry

There is only *one worry*, and that is, if we ourselves are stopping still. A man died if he never 'pushed on' from one of those resting places the dragoman prepared on an Eastern journey. They were not meant to be permanent. We must press on and on till we are transformed into the likenesss of Christ himself, and that is unlikely to be on this side of eternity. Only in eternity does finality exist.

THE ASCENSION DAY

In praise of human nature

> Acts 1.10–11 *'And while they were looking steadfastly into heaven as he went up, behold, two men stood by them in white apparel; which also said, "Ye men of Galilee, why stand ye looking into heaven?"'*

I could tell them. I'm not boasting, but I could tell those two angels why the Apostles on the Ascension Mount were looking steadfastly into heaven as Jesus went. I do not count it a hard question. *I* should look steadfastly if someone whom I loved, man or woman, was departing from me in a manner which seemed as final as this. I should stand there, I know I should, looking steadfastly till the water stood in my eyes. I hate 'goodbyes'.

But maybe, after all, I *don't* know the answer. Maybe I'm reading this too much through my own human feelings. Maybe these Apostles saw through the temporal nature of this event into its eternal significance. Maybe this is why in the account of the Ascension at the close of St. Luke's Gospel, the Apostles returned from this departure scene not with tears in their eyes, but with joy in their hearts. St. Luke says, 'And they worshipped him, and returned to Jerusalem with great joy: and were continually in the Temple, blessing God.'

They couldn't, of course, see *the other end* of the Ascension journey. They couldn't see the *arrival* in that place whither he had gone. Or could they? Perhaps they could with the eye of faith see what they could not see with natural sight, and if not then, maybe in days to come.

> See the Conqueror mounts in triumph,
> See the King in royal state
> Riding on the clouds his chariot
> To his heavenly palace gate:
> (Bishop Christopher Wordsworth 1862)

But if not then, on the Ascension Mount, did they, I wonder, come to see what the seer on Patmos saw?

'And I saw, and I heard the voice of many angels round about the throne and living creatures and the elders; and the number of them was ten thousand times ten thousand, and thousands of thousands; saying with a great voice, "Worthy is the Lamb that hath been slain to receive power, and riches, and wisdom, and might and honour, and glory, and blessing."'

I think they did come to see that, but not then, not on the first Ascension Day. They stood there, just as many of us stand now, moved, perhaps, bewildered perhaps, silent perhaps. There seems nothing to say. Jesus came. His was a lovely life, lovely in its never failing thought for others . . . but we must queue for the 'nine' bus in the morning, or wonder where to find ten feet of space in which to park our car. There may be difficult letters on our desk tomorrow. And someone is ill. And someone can't continue in the flat much longer, now that rents are rising. So we stand here in London's West End wondering like the Apostles of old at first, wondering what significance, if any, the Ascension of Christ can have for us.

1. *Christ is King*

First, I think, it can tell us all that Christ is King.

A little time ago, I read a striking book by E. P. Tisdall called *Restless Consort*. It was a study of him after whom this road where our church stands is named. It opened my eyes. No longer could I harbour in my mind vague notions of the Prince's inability wholly to fit into our British way of life. I learned instead how many of the achievements of the mid-Victorian age, like the great Exhibition of 1851, the Royal College of Science, and the organization of the Army were, in fact, the creation of Albert's fertile mind. His was the genius behind a great many of the reforms and advances achieved in his day. In fact, in no small measure he reigned behind the Victorian throne for the betterment of British life. We owe him, I have come to believe, a debt which in our minds we have never wholly paid.

In some such way as this, I think, Christ reigns behind the world we see. I know this may not be apparent on the surface. I know the Marxists reckon economic forces are the governing factor. I know that Freud and many like him reckon sex the swaying force in modern life. And there is fashion, custom and tradition. But behind all, and under all, and over all, I believe that what is represented by the one word 'Christ' is the final arbiter. Take away goodness from the world, and what framework is left to hold it up! If there were no purity, there could be no dirt. If there were no kindness, we should not know what hatred was. If there were no Christ, what final yardstick should we have to measure man's behaviour? That is why I say that in the last resort Christ reigns. It is the message of Ascension-tide. Our Lord is on the throne. Goodness holds the reigns of government.

2. *The destiny of our human nature*

Secondly, we see it was our human nature Jesus took on high. I would like us to think about this. Sometimes we half despise our human nature. We show we do by the words we use. We say, 'It's only human nature!' That is what we say when one of us commits some sin in the flesh, or is ruthless with his neighbour, or biting with his tongue. We say, 'You can't expect behaviour like an angel. I'm only human after all!'

But this human nature Jesus took on high. It is one of the greatest truths of the ascension. No longer can we despise our human nature. No longer can we excuse our human nature, or apologize for it. It was what God chose to assume in the Incarnation, and what Christ chose to elevate to God's eternal throne in heaven. Or as Bishop Wordsworth wrote:

> He has raised our human nature
> On the clouds to God's right hand;
> There we sit in heavenly places,
> There with him in glory stand:
> Jesus reigns, adored by angels;
> Man with God is on the throne;
> Mighty Lord, in thine Ascension
> We by faith behold our own.

But look what sides there are in human nature. We have read in the newspapers about Eichmann, one willing to indulge in genocide, an attempt to exterminate a whole race of men—the Jews: to send them trooping in thousands to the gas chambers: to pick out little children from Lidice, and to practise on their bodies fantastic experiments in the name of science. Again and again in history, human nature has sunk to deeds of shame.

And yet there is another side, an attractive side. There is not one of us who does not know of the simple goodness of human nature. Of parents sacrificing for their children. Of strangers giving help to strangers. Even of children crudely offering words of sympathy. I think of a little ten-year-old, to whom I sometimes speak in the street, blushing deeply, and hesitating long, yet sending me this message when she knew I was ill—'Please give him my love.' That, too, is human nature.

Human nature is not, according to Christian thought, some sordid, shallow, sinful thing. It is capable of the utmost nobility, depth and loveliness. To show us *this* Christ took it to his throne in heaven. That is why I call myself a Christian humanist. The Ascension puts a premium on our human nature.

3. *The divine sympathy*

And thirdly, it tells us that on the throne of heaven is One who understands us through and through. And not only understands but sympathizes. I sometimes wonder if in all the world there is any more strengthening relationship between two people than that of sympathetic understanding. And this is what after the ascension we know the God in heaven is like—a God of sympathetic understanding.

Agnes Turnbull in her novel *The Bishop's Mantle*, makes the hero of her story, a young American clergyman, answer the call of a wealthy industrialist, whose son had just taken his own life. It was one of those parish visits so difficult to make, the kind that saps your strength, and leaves you wondering what you have to offer. And sure enough he found the father almost broken up by what his son had done—its suddenness, its weakness, its grim finality. But deep down in his heart, the thought that troubled him most was this—What did *God* think of his son? And the young clergyman helped him there, helped by showing how he, a *human* father, was sympathetic to his boy, quoting then the words I've used myself in similar circumstances—'Like as a father pitieth his own children, even so is the Lord merciful to them that fear him'.

And this is the message of Ascensiontide. The God who reigns on high is a King of sympathetic understanding. It is the message of the Epistle to the Hebrews, 'Thy throne, O God, is for ever and ever', and 'We have not an high priest who cannot be touched with the feeling of our infirmities.'

There is of course the problem of thinking of God as if he were 'up there'. It has been so pressed on us that some of us dare scarcely speak about the Ascension. It is of course true that not all the statements in the Apostles' Creed can be taken in the same way as those referring to historical fact, like 'Suffered under Pontius Pilate'. 'Sitteth on the right hand of God the Father Almighty' is different. It points to a truth in mythological form. Perhaps the whole of what we call the Ascension is similar. It is certainly at the frontier point between historical truth and mythological truth. But it is still truth. And because it is truth, it has a message we ought to hear, and what it is, I have tried to outline.

THE ASCENSION DAY

The High God

INTRODUCTION

Before Mr. Kruschev left office he made a provocative remark which went round the world. The occasion was the triumph of one of Russia's astronauts. He said that when the astronaut was circling round the globe up there in space, he saw no signs of God anywhere about.

1. *The sky God*

Of course Mr. Kruschev was indulging in a little polite mockery in the presence of Russia's technological achievement, but in any case he was right; since the dawn of human history men have associated the divine presence either *with* the sky, or located it *in* the sky.

We should not be far wrong if we asserted that the early Hebrews probably thought like this about God. Perhaps such phrases as we sing in the Psalms are indicative, 'He that dwelleth in the heavens shall laugh them to scorn', though probably by the time they were incorporated in the Hebrew Psalter they were understood in a spiritual way. The reason for saying this is that the opening words of the Bible, dated perhaps in the sixth century B.C. demolished in a few words any idea of God coinciding with the sky. 'In the beginning God made the heavens and the earth.' So God must have existed before there were any heavens at all. He does not *belong* to the sky.

At about the same time, the Greeks, too, were thinking these problems out, and the Platonists among them came to assert that God has no position in any part of three-dimensional space. The most real Reality is not spatial at all.

Then by about the dawn of the Christian era, these two views, the Hebrew and the Greek, were combined, and it was openly taught, at least by one Hellenistic Jew, that the Old Testament language about God's hands, Gods eyes and God's voice was purely figurative.

The first point we are able to make then, is that although men used to think of God as up there in the sky, they began to refine these ideas at least two thousand five hundred years ago.

2. *Why the idea of height is retained as a symbol*
Although thinking men abandoned the idea of God as associated with the sky, the symbol of height connected with God has been retained because it conveys meaning.

Here are five reasons taken from Edwyn Bevan's book *Symbolism and Belief.*

(*a*) Height means *extra power*. Think of a man six feet five inches high swinging an axe.
(*b*) Height means *extra vision*. Think of a sailor climbing to a mast-head.
(*c*) Height involves a *sense of awe*. Think of a towering mountain.
(*d*) Height, or the sky, is the *source of light*. Down in the ground, as for example, a mine, it is dark.
(*e*) The sky suggests *order*. It was from watching the stars that the impulse for the scientific method arose.

Because men wanted to imply the authority of God in power and vision, because they wanted to assert his awesomeness, his illuminating power and his orderliness, they applied to him one revealing word, they talked about his *height*. 'O praise the Lord of heaven, praise him in the height.'

Some people say that this refining of the idea of height indicates that the notion of God is altogether a relic of primitive thinking. But because the calculations of the computer are a development from primitive man counting on his fingers and toes, are mathematics fanciful?

Surely the truth is men have been able to perceive more clearly what is the nature of God as the mists of time have lifted.

3. *God reveals himself*

The idea of God being gradually perceived through the mists is only partly true. This is because God is not an impassive object, but an active being. He comes to make himself known. He reveals himself. How? The answer is in Jesus of Nazareth. The hidden God becomes the revealed God. This is the Gospel. This is the good news. In the man Jesus, we see God close-up.

What line, then, do we take over God as 'height' when we wish to speak of him revealing himself? We say 'he came down.' And when that period of revelation in flesh was ended, what do we say? 'He went up. He ascended.' Not that he literally *came down* at Christmas. Not that he literally *went up* at the Ascension, as today's Gospel says. As the word 'height' is kept as a symbol, so the coming down and going up are kept as symbols. And most expressive symbols they are when we understand what they are expressing.

APPLICATION

We abandon this idea of height at our peril. Modern life is flat, as flat as materialism can make it. Of going *down*, we indeed know something. Going down to drug addiction, theft, abortion, promiscuity and homosexuality, in other words, degradation. But we need to rise up. We need to give time to the spiritual Reality that towers high up over all that is mundane, flat and earthy. This is done by worship. Worship is what lifts people. Absence of worship is what keeps people's eyes raking the ground. We need worship. We need it today. This is the message of the Ascension. Our desperate need of worship of the Most High.

SAINT BARNABAS THE APOSTLE

The man for the job

Acts 11.22 'And they sent forth Barnabas . . .'

I wish you could read Greek! Perhaps you can. If so you will know my text reads 'and they apostled Barnabas'. That is why we can call him an Apostle, although he was not one of 'the twelve'. But why pick on Barnabas? Why send him forth as a kind of Church plenipotentiary? The answer is, because he was the man for the job.

1. *A new situation*

The Church at Jerusalem was puzzled. News had reached its ears that the unprecedented step had been taken of proclaiming the Gospel to non-Jews in the Greek-speaking city of Antioch. What is more, there had been a considerable response. Quite a few people of foreign extraction were openly confessing themselves followers of Jesus. And as if that were not enough, the whole enterprise was unofficial. No-one had been commissioned to visit Antioch. The Church there (if you could call it a Church), had no Apostolic foundation. It had been founded by laymen who journeyed there as a result of a persecution. Who could be sure then it was a proper Christian faith the people in Antioch were professing? Who could say if the congregation in this city could be called 'The Church in Antioch'? Jerusalem needed to know the answers to these questions. They needed someone to go and make investigation. So they chose Barnabas. He seemed to be the man for the job.

2. A liberal-minded man

Why was Barnabas the man for the job? The account in the book of the Acts of the Apostles says 'he was a good man, and full of the Holy Ghost, and of faith'. He would need to be, otherwise he would never be fair to what he saw in Antioch, or able to read the signs of the Holy Spirit's working or recognize faith when he saw it. But we can add more from other hints we are given about Barnabas. He was generous, not only with his money (and he had a little), but in his judgements. He had an open mind. He could be called liberal, that is to say, he was ready for new situations and open to fresh ideas. And all this was tied to an evangelistic purpose in his life. It is to the Jerusalem Church's everlasting credit that they sent such a man as Barnabas to investigate the 'goings-on' in Antioch, and not a tight-lipped traditionalist. And so it turned out that Barnabas reported approval of the new things he saw. What is more, he searched out and brought in Saul of Tarsus to build up the work in Antioch. And as if this wasn't enough, out from Antioch Barnabas and Saul set sail on their missionary tours to other Gentile cities. Barnabas was the man for the job, and he discovered Saul, another man for the job.

3. The leaders we need

We need more Christians like Barnabas, generous men, generous in sympathy, generous in outlook, generous with their possessions. The Church expands when its members are outward-looking and not inward-looking, and unafraid of new situations. We must remember that the Holy Spirit is the Spirit of adventure, creating order out of chaos, and bringing light into darkness. Barnabas was a man full of the Holy Spirit. There are few men in the New Testament more attractive than he. In our changing world let us pray that God will keep the Church leaders alive to the opportunities in new situations, in other words, men for the job, men for the times.

SAINT BARNABAS THE APOSTLE

Maintaining the friendship

St. John 15.14 *'Ye are my friends, if ye do whatsoever I command you.'*

This sounds odd. Friends do not usually give each other commands and if they do, the friendship is soon abandoned. This verse might sound more reasonable if it read 'Ye are my *servants* if ye do whatsoever I command you.' This, however, is not what our Lord said. What is more, he made a point of emphasizing the fact that he does not call his disciples 'servants' but 'friends.' We must, therefore, try to understand his meaning.

1. *Sharing*

First of all, we are called friends because we are not left in the dark about our Lord's inmost life. This is not the case in the master–servant relationship. There, the master presents a façade, he maintains a distance, he keeps his counsel. Our Lord, however, *shared* with the twelve his life of utter dependence on his heavenly Father, whose will he perfectly trusted. And this even involved sharing with them his temptations. What could be more inward, personal and intimate! Not only did these twelve men share Jesus' exterior life, they were admitted to as much of his interior life as they were able to experience. He said, 'All things that I have heard of my Father I have made known unto you.'

2. *Chosen*

Our Lord also *chose* the twelve. A man who is chosen is conscious of a different relationship from one who has merely 'signed on'. The latter might not even be noticed. A girl might be a devoted admirer of a man, but what a difference when he chooses her to share life with him. Some people find this idea of God choosing his followers difficult, especially when it appears as the doctrine of election. The sting, however, is taken out of it when we understand that the election is not for privilege but for service. 'I have chosen you . . . that ye should go and bring forth fruit', said Jesus. Choice for service is still choice. It still produces a warmth of personal relationship, and this is the relationship that exists between God and his people; it can be summed up in the word 'friends'.

3. *The moral bond*

But what about these formidable sounding commands 'Ye are my friends if ye do whatsoever I command you'? We may look at the matter this way, How can two people be friends if their approach to life is totally different? Similarly, our status of friendship with God rests on a moral bond. First, God forgives us our sins and restores us to a personal relationship with him. Many times we fail to live up to this privilege. Again and again we need the divine forgiveness and again and again it is granted, but if in spite of our failings we really want to do God's will, that is, do what he commands, our friendship stands secure. It is what we long in our heart of hearts to do that maintains the friendship. It does so because it maintains the personal intimacy. In a sense it is not our sins that break the friendship, what breaks it is refusing to acknowledge them in God's presence, so as to receive his forgiveness. It is we who make the break not our sins and certainly not God.

4. *Keeping the friendship intact*

It would be a proper attitude to the Holy Communion on St. Barnabas' Day to see it as a means of keeping our friendship with our Lord intact. Barnabas had a peculiar gift for friendship. This was one of his strong points. So it is right to think about friendship today and in particular *our acceptance of Christ's friendship*. See how I have turned this last phrase. I have done it on purpose.

SAINT JOHN BAPTIST'S DAY

A voice in the wilderness

Isaiah 40.3 'The voice of him that crieth in the wilderness.'

From the road it looked a fine house and as it seemed to be open to the public I made my way up the drive. But what a shock was in store. The garden was a wilderness. The herbaceous borders were overgrown. The York paved terrace was almost covered with moss. The climbing roses on the house itself had been allowed to climb up to the gutters.

The surprising fact about John the Baptist is that he chose such an environment from which to speak out his message. His was a voice in the wilderness. I say *chose* because he could have spoken from the ordered life of his father's priestly home. Instead he chose to be a prophet in the wilderness. Why? We may give three reasons.

1. Because ordered life is not enough

Too often we think it adequate. All the country needs is the discipline of good homes, the training of modern schools, the ordered round of the Church's year of worship. And none of these things is to be despised. They are not even dispensable. Certainly they cannot be rated as luxuries. What they do not, however, produce is *transformed* life. All they produce is *regulated* life. And should the regulations be weakened, or their pressure relaxed, a looseness exhibits itself surprising to many. Such is the strength and weakness of what St. Paul called 'the Law'.

2. Because men listen in the wilderness

They have to listen. The disappointing outcome of the ordered life is so shattering they are ready to hear some word of God. So the prophet speaks in the wilderness. He speaks where all our tidy schemes for moral and social betterment lie in tangled ruins. Men have to be converted from themselves to God before they are built up on a sure foundation. All this is devastating to personal pride. Man has to be unhitched from the centre of his own individual concern and refashioned with God as the centre of his hopes. All this spoils his petty plans. That is why God speaks to him from a place of devastation.

3. *Because God's purpose is for transformed people*

His aim is not for self-centred persons nor for desolation, tears and disappointment, but for lives rebuilt on a sure foundation. What the prophet speaks, then, in the wilderness is good news, hopeful news, recreating news. 'O thou that bringest good tidings to Zion . . . Behold, the Lord God will come with a strong hand, and his arm shall rule for him.'

To hear this word the crowds of ordinary folk in Judea and Galilee for whom the law-abiding had little sympathy collected. A recreating word is every man's deep need.

CONCLUSION

Let us thank God for such ordered upbringing as has profited us, but let us rely rather on the grace which comes to us through Christ in Word and Sacrament, able to build us up on a more secure basis than the barrenness of our self-centred personalities.

SAINT JOHN BAPTIST'S DAY

A child of promise

St. Luke 1.66 '*What manner of child shall this be?*'

The accent in this sentence should fall on the last word; and all because the question is not so much an enquiry as an expression of wonder. An exclamation mark would be more appropriate than a query. In this situation no answer was expected, only time would tell, and time did tell.

1. *The potentialities in every child*

Of course this is true for every baby. You see him kicking his legs in the perambulator and you do not know if he will become Prime Minister some day, or the country's representative at the Olympic Games. He doesn't appear as either kind of person, but who knows? Mrs. Sutherland in Australia had no idea that the little girl in her arms would one day be thrilling sophisticated audiences at Covent Garden, l'Opéra in Paris and La Scala in Milan. You never know what a child will turn out to be.

2. *John the Baptist's background*

It was the *circumstances* of John the Baptist's birth that formed the question which was an exclamation, 'What manner of child shall this *be*?' There had been a proclamation by an angel, so the scripture says in its poetic way. And a miraculous pregnancy by a woman beyond her time. And a father made speechless by his doubts (that really is unusual). And the name 'John' had never been used in the family. And the father not only recovered his speech with the naming of the child, he spoke out in prophecy. 'This child will bring about the mercy promised to our fathers.' A child of promise indeed!

3. *The importance of the home*

Every child is a child of promise. Not all, however, fulfil the early promises. We can, however, increase the opportunities for fulfilment. We can see that the homes into which our children are born are homes of Christian faith and practice. We can make sure that the parents themselves live out the behaviour they wish their children to exhibit. Children should be taken to Church, not sent to Church. And they should be incorporated by baptism into that sphere where the opportunities for the grace of God to be effective are enhanced.

What manner of child shall this be? No-one knows for certain. But in the God-fearing home the possibilities for greatness are increased a hundred-fold. It was when the neighbours looked at John the Baptist's home that they exclaimed 'What manner of child shall this *be*?' The faith of the parents holds the secret of their child's possibilities more than does the school, the neighbourhood or the money available.

APPLICATON

When we kneel at the Lord's table today, we could spend some time praying for our homes, and our children too, if we have them, for they come after us.

SAINT PETER'S DAY

The Church in prison

Acts 12.5 *'Peter therefore was kept in prison: but prayer was made without ceasing of the church unto God for him.'*

I would like you to imagine for a moment that you are in the old city of Jerusalem, that place of so much cruelty, hate and bloodshed, all mixed with idealism and religious aspiration. I would like you to imagine that you are in one of those narrow alleyways where small windows, perched high up on the walls of the flanking houses, suggest dark interiors. And presently you come to an iron gate, strong and forbidding; and with your eye fixed to a tiny aperture in it you see through to another gate beyond, of similar stoutness. And then it dawns on you that what you see is Jerusalem's prison, grim and frightening, like prisons throughout the world. And could you have peered inside on the day focused in the words of my text, you would have seen an Apostle there, the chief Apostle, the man who represented the official Church, which was why he was there. St. Peter, seized by Herod,. the representative of the State. 'Peter therefore was kept in prison; but prayer was made without ceasing of the Church unto God for him.'

Peter had done no wrong. He had, in fact, been incarcerated because Herod had it in mind to harry the Church. So he seized James the brother of John, and had him run through with a sword. Just like that. No trial. No accusation, at least, none of any significance. And then, because the murder pleased the public, Peter was seized also. And now you see him, in imagination at least, sitting chained, guarded by soldiers, waiting his end. Peter the big fisherman from Galilee, used to the open sky.

1. The Church in prison

I think the official Church is in prison today, sitting there in chains, locked behind stout bars. It is not the State that is responsible. No official action has been taken. We do not even know anti-clericalism in this country. But two other modern powers have laid their hands upon the official Church and got it shackled, manacled and rendered all but ineffective in a corner. I refer to over-organization and to secularization.

Let me explain what I mean.

First, over-organization. Tomorrow there will come into London from all over England members of what is called the Church Assembly, meeting from Monday till Friday at Westminster, about seven hundred of them, clergy, including bishops, and laity. This happens twice every year. This week there are seventy-nine items on their agenda, not counting possible amendments, some of them matters of great complexity. The frightening fact is the amount of time, talent and money that will be locked up again this week in the official debating chamber at Church House, Westminster, most of it having little obvious connection with the mission of the Church to the people of London and England, and will have little practical effect on the Christianizing of this nation, at a time when she sorely needs it. It is easy to blame the Church itself, or this person or that group, but what has happened is that the Church has got caught in the clutches of the demon of organization which is everywhere in the world today, so that we are swamped in elections, committees, sub-committees, reports and resolutions; a veritable deluge of paper and manilla files, a great deal of it in the name of democracy. And here sits the Church, walled in by organization, a prisoner locked within its own procedure. And all the time, the thought keeps running through the minds of some of us that the Church was stronger in numbers and stronger in influence when it had no Church Assembly, no central oraganization, and no Church House in Westminster at all. And it may be that the ordinary man today sees the Church captured by the same system which has also captured him, how then can it deliver him or speak to him? And that is why he has so little sympathy with *organized* religion, I said organized. . . .

Secondly, *secularization*. This also has imprisoned the Church. I could be misunderstood over this, as I could be over organization, as if I were in favour of formlessness, and this is not true. I could also be misunderstood over secularization, as if I were in favour of a Church-dominated society, which I am not. I agree with the most modern thought on this, that we have to recognize and accept the secular world, that is all that area of life, and it is considerable, which is subject to the scientific method of approach. It is God's world. But in a sense it runs on its own. It is also able to be mastered by man as man. But the secular has got a man in prison when he comes to think that the secular is all. He must remember that there is that which transcends the secular, the area of the personal is an example, and it is in that transcendent sphere that religion operates and the unprecedented and unexpected may happen. But the trouble is, the modern Church has got itself imprisoned. That is why the Church seems pointless, useless and irrelevant in modern society. Men leave it to itself. Only if there is a qualitative difference about the Church has it any point. Only if it shakes itself free from the modern mood of how little can I believe and still be called a Christian. Jesus said, 'According to your faith, so be it unto you.' If we believe little we shall accomplish little. If we believe much, if we believe in the supernatural we shall accomplish much. But for the Church at the moment, this involves rising up and leaving a prison. Will it happen? If it doesn't, we can expect little from it in the way of renewal.

CONCLUSION

I come back to my text. 'Peter therefore was kept in prison: but prayer was made without ceasing of the church unto God for him.' We can picture the situation. All over Jerusalem, up other alleyways than the one in which the prison stood, behind some of those windows high up the walls of the flanking buildings, little groups of men and women knelt praying for Peter. 'Lord, give us back Peter. Lord, bring Peter out of prison. Lord, give deliverance to thy Church in this our time of need.'

Does it happen in London today? Does it happen in Kensington? Does it happen in this parish? Oh yes, there will be criticism. The Church is bogged down in organization! The Church is gripped by the spirit of the age and is powerless. And these criticisms are partly true. But how many will pray for the Church? 'Lord, deliver thy Church from her bondage. Lord, set it free, give it the strength to rise up and shake off its shackles of "this-worldness." '

And you turn back to the twelfth chapter of the Book of the Acts of the Apostles and read of Peter at the eleventh hour rising up from the prison, his manacles falling off, and his passing through those terrifying iron gates and joining the praying company, to their utter astonishment.

APPLICATION

Shall *we* pray for the Church today, the official Church? Perhaps we half think it is past praying for. Miracles can happen. We need the Church today, and a Church that believes in prayer, the power of God and the strength of faith, hope and love. It is the only kind of Church we need, the only kind worth belonging to. . . .

SAINT PETER'S DAY

The great confession

Matthew 16.16 (NEB) '*Simon Peter answered "You are the Messiah, the Son of the living God."* '

Not so very long ago the Television programme *Panorama* turned its attention to the Church of England. It was not unsympathetic, nor was it markedly in favour, it could even be said to be attempting an objective presentation. It showed, for instance, a sensible and good-looking young vicar in the north of England obtaining some considerable response to his ministry; he was open to new ideas, yet wise enough not to throw away everything that was old just because it was old. The programme also presented rather an old-fashioned looking garden fête, rather dull and not the sort of event likely to attract the young today. Then there followed an interview with a determined looking middle-aged vicar who was confident that the Church's troubles were due to its apparent inhibitions over talking about God. Next came a 'progressive' type who told us how he had modernized his church, turning some of its premises into an efficient welfare organization, including an up-to-date canteen, but it did not bring the people to church. He was in consequence against church buildings, and would only keep places like St. Paul's Cathedral and Westminster Abbey for the 'big occasions'.

1. *The Church's foundation task*

Today's Gospel reminds us that the Church's *foundation task* is to make its conviction known about Jesus of Nazareth. St. Peter answered 'You are the Messiah, the Son of the living God.' To this our Lord made reply, 'You are Peter the rock; and on this rock I will build my Church.' The Church is built on the rock of the ordinary man, of whom Peter was typical, making the great confession about Jesus. This is the distinctive thing the Church has to say and through which it exists. If it cannot, or does not do this, it will not survive. Sometimes it seems as if the Church has entertained the muddled notion that its foundation task is to provide a welfare service, only to run into disappointment because it is outstripped by what the State can supply. The Church, however, exists to bear testimony to a distinctive conviction about Jesus. No-one else will do it. And if the Church makes anything else primary it will fail.

2. Confession by word and by life

How does the Church carry out the foundation task? By preaching, of course, and by speaking. These ways are never superseded, but it is not by words only. The Lordship of Jesus is proclaimed by the life of the community of believers that follow his way. It is a distinctive way. It is at many points quite different from the worldly way. For example, it is the way of the Cross; it is the way that seeks to overcome not by force but by love; it is the way of giving and not of getting; it is the way of steadfastness and not of shiftiness, the way of charity and not of fault-finding. For a community to live in this fashion, and for individuals to embody it in practice, is to proclaim the Lordship of Jesus over our common life.

APPLICATION

The great question is to ask what is the great priority. If this is clear and is acted upon, other activities in the life of the Church will fall into their proper place, but not otherwise. The great confession is the great rock-like basis. The great rock-like basis is the great confession. It is to make sure that all the Church does is squarely built at this point that the Gospel for Saint Peter's Day is set.

SAINT JAMES THE APOSTLE

The antidote to pointlessness

Acts 12.2 'And he killed James the brother of John with a sword.'

It all seemed so swift, so sudden and so final. There was the gleam of the sharpened steel, the thrust, and it was all over. 'And he killed James, the brother of John with a sword.'

1. *Questions without answers*

But was it all over? Was it all over for James? We who keep his day, July 25th, don't think so. We think *his name* lives for evermore. He was a Christian martyr. We think *he* lives for evermore. The redemption by Christ has taken him into its great refashioning sweep. Almost the very last words we have recited today in our service were, 'And I look for the resurrection of the dead, and the life of the world to come.' No, it wasn't all over for James, the brother of John, when Herod killed him with a sword.

But was it all over for Salome, the mother of James? I mean, was the incident over? Was the pain over? Was the questioning over? Was the doubt over? Some of you are mothers. You put yourself in Salome's shoes. 'And he killed James, the brother of John with a sword.' That is what Herod did. Why? Because he saw that it would please the Jews! And so there lay James' crumpled, bleeding, broken body for no deeper reason than politics. Herod thought a Christian's death would please the Jews.

There are some deaths over which we cannot grieve, wonder or agonise. An old lady dies, full of years, full of pain now, full of limitations. Who can lament her passing?

A man, not so old, dies. He has worn himself out in some good cause. Now, because of him, some new enterprise is helping forward other men. We lament his loss. We miss him sorely. But there is some reason for his death. No-one can say his departure is completely lacking of accomplishment.

But what about James? Killed for politics. Killed for a whim. Killed just for the sake of 'trying it on'. I say, 'Put yourself in Salome's shoes.' It was the senselessness, the pointlessness, the utter barrenness of it all that kept on hurting, hurting as the days went by.

And there was that road accident last week. What did it achieve? What did it produce? What did it initiate? The man was in the prime of life. It is the senselessness, the pointlessness, the utter barrenness of all loss of life through accidents that hurts. Those bathing fatalities that occur round our coasts every summer. . . . Those plane crashes. . . .

And then think how Salome saw Herod seize Peter after the death of her own son. Perhaps she ran to comfort Peter's wife; perhaps she ran to the mother-in-law. But then what happened? Peter was sleeping in prison between two soldiers, bound with two chains. And God stretched forth his hand and delivered Peter from the jaws of that death! Put yourself in Salome's shoes. God delivered Peter. He did not deliver her son. He let Herod kill 'James, the brother of John with a sword'.

There are some questions which cannot be answered on any basis of knowledge whatsoever. As a woman said to me one day, 'My neighbour's three sons went to the war, they all came back. My only son also went. He did not come back. If there is a God, why?'

2. Faith, the only approach

We can only answer this kind of question out of faith, there is no other way. I mean by this, we can look first squarely into what we are taught by the Gospel that God is not cruel, not forgetful, and not powerless, and not without our human fund of common kindness. I say we must look first at that, long and hard, we *must* look at it. And then when the image has become firmly printed upon the canvas of our minds, we must look at James, crumpled there on the floor of his prison, killed by Herod with a sword, allowed by God to be killed.

God's love was not suspended then. God's care was not suspended then. God's purposes were not frustrated then. There is no other outcome but pointlessness if we do not hold on to this.

This is what I am afraid of in our modern world, where faith in the existence of God at all, let alone a God of love, is weakening. I am afraid of pointlessness. Pointlessness stamping its ugly seal on everything. What is the use of trying? What is the use of working? What is the use even of living in a world like ours.

Such is the drain to which meaninglessness drives us, meaning-lessness about everything that comes our way.

Not long ago I carried out a visit I had been dreading. Inquiries had been made into the activities of a man I knew. They dragged on for months. Then the trial. It ran into weeks. Last of all, the verdict. The man was pronounced guilty, and the sentence of imprisonment was passed. I called on the wife the day after he was taken away. I say I dreaded my visit. I expected bitterness, resentment, a determination to appeal, the beginnings of a break-up of all purposeful living. She had had a bad twenty-four hours, but when I met her she spoke quietly about the meaning of Easter, and how it at least showed that in God's view, good can come out of evil. 'We must see life, our life like that', she said . . . I could scarcely believe my ears, sitting there in her flat, but I knew as I heard it that a general pointlessness of life would not drag her down, because of the calamity that had befallen them—her faith would see her through.

It would be strange if there were not some among us who at some time or other did not doubt the love of God because of what had happened to us. I expect that experience came to Salome when Herod killed James, the brother of John with a sword. And she was the mother of an Apostle! But I expect the fellowship of the Church to which she belonged kept her in the faith by holding her at that time tightly in the fellowship. That is what a congregation can do for the bereaved. So she found her balance once more. She kept her hold on the love of God which does not ever break.

3. *An act of service*

But it is of St. James we must think today, and not chiefly of his mother. St. James, who with that energetic temperament of his had cried out for some heavy task to perform for Jesus' sake. God had granted his prayer, though not in the way he expected. He had given him the task of paying the highest price for his discipleship, the price of life laid down. We do not always see as we should that to suffer persecution, ostracism and rejection may be the greatest service we each can render. To suffer it without hitting back. It may be that it is to this service now that the whole Church is being called. We are being attacked, but we must remember Christ gave his life a ransom for many, as the Gospel for today tells us. St. James, too, gave his life. Herod killed him with a sword. Our life, our discipleship, our Churchmanship is not pointless if we take our adversities patiently, by keeping hold of the love of God in Christ, which never breaks. It is achieving purposes beyond what we can ever imagine.

SAINT JAMES THE APOSTLE

What prayer is not

Matthew 20.21 (NEB) *'I want you'*, *she said*, *'to give orders that in your kingdom my two sons here may sit next to you, one at your right and the other at your left.'*

INTRODUCTION

What a way to begin! What a way to approach Christ! Listen to the words again. 'I want you to give orders that in your kingdom. . . .' Do you indeed! Who was this approaching with such bold effrontery, making her demands? It was a woman, a mother. It was in fact Jesus' aunt, the sister of Jesus' mother. And at once we draw our conclusions. Salome (for that was her name), Salome reckoned that because of the family tie she could order Jesus about. Or perhaps you add to that your own opinions as to the lengths mothers will sometimes go to push the claims of their sons. Here, you say was a proud, possessive, pushing mother. And you may be right. I don't know. But I notice that when Jesus answered he did not answer *her*. He answered instead the two sons. And my guess is that it was they who had put her up to it. 'Mother', they said, 'look, you've got some standing over Jesus, you remember when he was a child in arms, you are his aunt. He must listen to you. *You* ask him. He can't refuse you. We want chief places in this kingdom which Jesus promises.' Yes, James and John were 'go-getters'. And James' name comes first. He was a 'go-getter'. And Salome fell in, not without pride, maybe. So we see the little deputation approach Jesus. (Apparently Zebedee the father kept out.) Salome bowed low and Jesus said 'What is your wish?' It was quite formal in its way. Then the words came tumbling out, straight, blunt and demanding. 'I want you to give orders that in your kingdom my two sons here may sit next to you, one at your right and the other at your left.'

Now when you think about this incident you see it is an illustration of prayer. A woman comes kneeling and asking Jesus for something. That is prayer. Only it is the wrong kind of prayer. It is the wrong *attitude* in praying. And that is how we shall look at this Epistle for St. James' Day, a lesson in what praying is *not*.

1. First, prayer is not bringing pressure to bear on God

Far too often we think it is as St. James thought it was, till he learned better. We think that if we can regiment a *number* of people to pray, the size of the group will determine its effectiveness, just as if God were more likely to react in proportion to the pounds of prayer pressure exerted on him. And of course it is all wrong.

And then there is what Jesus labelled a heathen attitude in prayer. Thinking that God will be worn down to grant our requests if we increase, not perhaps the number of people praying, but the length of time they pray. So we hear of prayers all night and chains of prayer, and in Tibet things called 'praying wheels', a mechanical device to keep the praying going.

And there are even some people who think they can exert a kind of psychological pressure through prayer if they 'claim' in their minds, so to speak, the answers to their prayers, falling back on some words of Jesus that when we pray we should believe we have the answers and then we shall receive them.

All this, however, amounts to a wrong conception of prayer. Prayer never is bringing pressure to bear on God. And if we do encourage a number of people to pray it is so that the sphere of God's activity in co-operating minds may be extended. And if we pray all night, it is in order to keep our sails hoisted to the divine wind the longer, so as to be impelled by his Spirit. And if we claim answers it is only in the general sense that he has promised to be gracious, and we claim that promise.

It really does not matter *how* we pray, standing up, sitting down, kneeling, crouching, intoning our prayers on G, saying them in the natural voice, or singing them to some musical arrangement. All that matters is that it shall be an effective means for keeping our human spirits open to the leading of God's Spirit. Then things happen.

2. *Secondly, we need to note that prayer is not made from a position of strength*

This again is where James went wrong, and his brother John, and Salome their mother. Perhaps Zebedee their father knew better, and that is why he did not join the deputation. The other members of the family, however, thought that because they were related by blood to Jesus, and Salome was a generation older anyway, that they were in a strong position.

But we are never in a strong position when it comes to praying. We are in a very weak position. And for this reason, that our knowledge is very limited. That is why we ought never to make demands in prayers. Here in this story, Salome and her two sons came full of bounce, asking for chief seats in the kingdom. Had they known then what they came to know later that coming into his kingdom meant for Jesus crucifixion with a robber at his right and a robber at his left, they would have torn their own tongues out before making request for *those* two places! No wonder Jesus replied 'You do not know what you are asking.'

And nor do we when we make *specific* requests in prayer. Prayer for success here. Prayer for recovery there. We do not know what we are asking. We always pray from a position of weakness. But God knows and God understands. He understands what is best even though all things are possible. So what we really should do when we come to pray is put our weakness in God's strength, and our limited understanding in God's infinite wisdom.

3. *Prayer has not failed when we receive the answer 'No' to our prayers*

I suppose James thought it had. And John likewise, and Salome into the bargain. Together they had fixed up this deputation hoping to get Jesus to do what they wanted, and they receive the answer 'No'. We are not told how they retreated from the appointment, but I guess there was not much 'light' in their step. They thought the prayer a failure.

But was it a failure? When Paul prayed that his thorn in the flesh, that frustrating epilepsy, or whatever it was, might be removed from his life, had his prayer failed because he received the answer 'No'? I don't think so. Paul was a much better Christian because he had to endure that trouble, because, as he himself came to see, it tempered the self-glorying to which he could so easily be prone. When God says 'No' to our prayers, this is an answer. And maybe the best answer. It was the best answer to James and John then, and to Salome. We must remember that God guides with closed doors as well as with open doors. We must learn to take the answers that come, and not call prayer a failure because what we want is not always given.

CONCLUSION

What then is prayer? We have been discovering what it is not. What is the positive answer? It is putting ourselves, putting some situation, putting someone else's need into God's hands and leaving it there. If only Salome had come to Jesus with her two sons saying 'Here we are, do with us what you will', what rejoicing there would have been on the part of

Christ, that this willing channel for the flow of his beneficial spirit was being made available. Perhaps they did learn to come like this later on. If so, that was the triumph of St. James, he had arrived at the place of humility in prayer, the only kind worth while.

SAINT BARTHOLOMEW THE APOSTLE

Fear and Power

1. *A powerful Church*

First impressions are important. This is true especially of our impressions of people. I remember a man applying for a job who struck me as spoilt and sulky. He got the job and I tried to change my opinion, but events proved that I had been right. The first impression the early Church gave was of power. This is the impression the portion of scripture appointed for the Epistle for today gives. A Church so evidently possessed of spiritual power that people crowded into the streets bringing their sick for healing, and they were not disappointed.

Is this the impression the Church today gives of itself? Does it seem to be pulsating with power? At one time it appeared to possess temporal power. It occupied a dominant place in society. Its buildings towered above other buildings in the neighbourhood. Today the Church is virtually powerless in all these senses. Even its cathedrals are overtopped by concrete blocks of offices and its position in society is marginal. That the Church has lost the power of prestige does not matter. The important question is, has it lost spiritual power? Is the first impression the Church gives today one of strong inner resources, or is it of a body timid, divided and morbidly unsure of itself?

2. A feared Church

If we look closer at our passage of scripture we shall note that not only did people crowd round the Church for healing, but some were so afraid of it they kept out of the way. Is anyone afraid of the Church now? Do we want them to be afraid of it? It all depends why these people in Jerusalem were afraid. The reason is because the Apostles, and particularly Peter, set up a standard of sincerity, as in the case of Ananias and Sapphira, not seen elsewhere.

3. The Church's inner strength

Purity and power go together. The Church that is crooked is the Church that is weak. The Church that is straight is the Church that is strong. When the Church exhibits the power of holiness, and first impressions count, men will fear it, and they will come to it for healing. The Church is a long way these days from being feared. It could be because it is insufficiently like Bartholomew (Nathanael), in whom we are told there was no guile. Purity means power and power produces respect and without respect no-one will come for healing.

SAINT BARTHOLOMEW THE APOSTLE

Snobbery

I hope I am not doing St. Bartholomew an injustice, but I wonder if he was a snob. Not a class snob, nor a financial snob, but a religious snob. I wonder this because when Philip burst in on Nathanael's devotions, (Bartholomew and Nathanael are probably identical), with the words. 'We have found him of whom Moses in the law and the prophets did write, Jesus of Nazareth, the son of Joseph', Nathanael's mind did not get beyond Nazareth. He saw the place in his mind's eye, undistinguished, unimaginative, small. No 'Nagels' nor 'Baedeker' would have listed it. 'Can any good thing' asked Bartholomew, 'come out of Nazareth?' expecting the answer, 'No'. That is the essence of snobbery. No room in the mind for anything outside its own preconceptions, no openness to the possibility of surprises, no breadth of vision. The trouble with Bartholomew was that he had closed his mind on Nazareth.

The Gospel for today opens by telling us of a dispute among the Apostles as to who was the greatest. Was Bartholomew to the fore in that dispute? Is this the reason why this passage of scripture has been chosen for today? Did Bartholomew pass disparaging remarks about practical religion? About faith in God which issued chiefly in service to other people's needs? About piety in which contemplation formed only a small part? We remember how he first appears in the Gospel records as meditating under a fig tree, probably on the saga of Jacob's dream of a ladder set up from earth to heaven. Bartholomew's religion was of the mystical, devotional, intellectual type. Did he despise other types? Did he count his own kind as the greatest? Was he a spiritual snob? a religious snob? Would he, in our day, have time only for a religious talk on 'Radio 3'? Would he be a Catholic of the type who has sympathy only for liturgical purity, regardless of people's needs? Would he be an Evangelical of the kind unable to see beyond the requirements of Reformation insights? Would he, in the fashion of mid-twentieth-century German demythologizing, despise those simple folk who count historicity as important in the Biblical records? Was Bartholomew not simply a religious intellectual—such can be a true follower of Christ—but a religious intellectual snob which is a distortion of discipleship of the Man from Nazareth?

What is wrong with snobbery?

1. It overlooks grace

It forgets or avoids St. Paul's question, 'What hast thou that thou didst not receive?' Human beings are not all equal in capacity, and if they were all made equal in possessions, their unequal capacity would soon result in unequal possessions. And we have not all an education of equal quality behind us, nor a family pedigree of like purity. It is stupid to meet these facts with attempts at denigration, asserting that they are not benefits. It is also wrong to treat them as acquirements through our merit if we possess them. If we examine their origin it will be found that they are gifts. How can a man be proud of a gift? This is the folly of snobbery.

2. *It overlooks service*

In the Bible there is a much misinterpreted doctrine called the doctrine of election. In particular, in Calvinism, as popularly understood, it came to stand for a massive injustice; some are elected to salvation, others to damnation, all through no merits or faults of their own. So the principle of 'by grace alone' became an affront to the human mind. All this came about through misreading the Biblical idea of election. There election is for service, not for privilege. Similarly, the gifts of God's spirit, according to St. Paul, are not even for the edifying of the individual Christian, but only for the building up of the congregation, the body of Christ; from which it follows that the possession of spiritual gifts cannot be taken as an indication of the degree of development of a Christian. Because all gifts are for the service of the community, snobbery is wrong. Did St. Bartholomew come to understand this? Did his petty pride in his personal possessions and status disappear like morning mist when he saw the Man from Nazareth give his life a ransom for many? Did the resurrection of Christ build up his personality at a new centre?

APPLICATION

To all of us guilty of snobbery, and it belongs to all classes, Jesus speaks in the words of today's Gospel, 'I am among you as he that serveth.' And we note the kind of service he pictured, the practical labour of serving others at table. Bartholomew must be ready for this. His contemplative life must not be counted an excuse. There is nothing we possess that is not ultimately a gift. There is nothing we have that is not to be put to the service of others. Only so are possessions and status safe. To this state of safety or salvation there is no doubt St. Bartholomew finally arrived, and in so doing he became Christ's true Apostle, one able to be sent forth as his representative, representative of the serving Man from Nazareth.

SAINT MATTHEW THE APOSTLE

Servants

2 Corinthians 4.5 (NEB) *'It is not ourselves that we proclaim; we proclaim Christ Jesus as Lord, and ourselves as your servants, for Jesus' sake.'*

INTRODUCTION

There was an unpleasant rumour going the rounds in the Church. Some people, of course, wouldn't hear of it, but others leant 'half an ear'. They whispered 'There is no smoke without fire.' And St. Paul 'got wind of it'. It was about himself and his fellow ministers in Corinth. The rumour was that they were deceivers, craftily twisting the Word of God to boost their own status. And before we begin dismissing this piece of New Testament as out of date, let us be aware of the fact that the Christian Church has constantly been open to the temptation to approach problems by asking first how they will affect the standing of the Church. Sometimes it has fallen to the temptation. Paul, however, stoutly refused this accusation, and in doing so made three points in defence of his ministry, which points still act as indications of what a proper ministry should be.

1. *Not a proclamation of the ministry*

St. Paul said, 'It is not ourselves that we proclaim.' At first this sounds too fantastic. What preacher would mount a pulpit to proclaim himself? But the situation is more subtle. All too easily the loose idea becomes current that the Church is the clergy. Sometimes we hear the phrase 'So and so entered the Church', that is, 'he became a clergyman'. When, therefore, a preacher proclaims that the Church is part of the Gospel, and it is, the impression could easily gain ground that he was proclaiming himself. To avoid any misunderstanding, Paul came down flat with his statement. It is not ourselves that we proclaim. The Church is not the clergy.

2. *Jesus as Lord is the proper proclamation*

When a wheel-tapper goes the length of a train as it stands at the platform or in the siding, tapping each wheel of each coach with his hammer, he appears casual in his work, he scarcely seems to be paying attention to what he is doing. In point of fact, however, he is noting the authentic ring his hammer makes on the metal tyre of the wheel, and if he does not hear it, he will examine the wheel, and if it appears cracked, expert opinion will be summoned and the train disallowed from continuing its journey.

Similarly, there is an authentic ring about preaching. It must bear testimony to the Lordship of Jesus. 'It is not ourselves that we proclaim', said Paul, 'but Christ Jesus as Lord.' Notice the name. Notice the use of the word 'Jesus'. Lordship is not ascribed simply to some inner mystical experience of Christ, but to the man Jesus of Nazareth, who walked about in Galilee, ate, drank, grew tired and went to sleep just as we do in dependence on God. If this Jesus come in the flesh does not figure in preaching, if *this* Jesus is not proclaimed as the Lord of life, no proper preaching is taking place, there is no authentic ring.

3. *The ministers as servants*

Jesus is the Lord, but he came as the servant. This, too, must be the bearing of all Christian ministers. They are not managing directors, they are not even chairmen, except at certain committee meetings. Their task is to serve people, and this means serving them from the pulpit as well as in welfare activities. Sometimes preaching gives its attention more to orthodoxy or the latest radical theory, or to ecclesiastical structural reforms, but the words of the minister in the pulpit as well as the deeds of the minister in the local old people's home are to serve the needs of the people, elementary and unintellectual as they may be. 'It is not ourselves that we proclaim; we proclaim Christ Jesus as Lord, and ourselves as your servants, for Jesus' sake.'

CONCLUSION

On St. Matthew's Day our thoughts run back to the man who sat at the receipt of custom, and was called by Jesus to follow him, and he did so. That act of renunciation involved abandoning a life in which under the old Roman system of tax gathering there was much cunning, distortion and lying for the sake of personal gain. At that receipt of custom the mind of the official was concerned mainly with what he could get out of it for himself. Such must never be the mind of the Church, her ministers or any of her members. Our task is to serve people in the name of the Lord Jesus, who though he was Lord came as a servant. This is what we need to remember today as we kneel together at the Lord's table. It is really the servants' table. The Lord was a servant, and we must be servants.

SAINT MATTHEW THE APOSTLE

The small undistinguished fishing village on the coast of Portugal carried my mind back to New Testament scenes. It could have been Galilee. Its name, Capernaum. The centre of activity was the water's edge. There on the beach was spread out the night's catch of fish displayed for sale. And the tax office was there prominently housed at the centre of activities. No haul of fish was made but the tax officer was involved, staking his claim. His name could have been Matthew.

There are three stages in today's Gospel, first, the break, second, the re-association, and thirdly, the proclamation. Each is important.

1. The break

We need only to imagine the scene. Every day was the same on the Capernaum waterfront. It had to be if life was to continue. Every night the catch of fish. Every morning the sale of fish. Every day the tax gatherer staking his claim. But one day he was missing. At least the familiar face was missing. If any one single person could have been chosen whose absence would be most noticeable, that man was the tax gatherer. Therefore Jesus picked out Matthew from the Capernaum community and said, 'Come, follow me.'

No profound thought is called for to estimate that Matthew had been stirred many times before this. He had listened to Jesus. Perhaps he had caught his eye. Anyway, Jesus knew that the time was not far distant when it needed only a command to Matthew, and he would quit that tax office for ever.

It has been my privilege in recent years to visit most of the theological colleges in England to talk to the students. A few days ago I was at Salisbury. There I met one who had been a policeman, another an officer in the merchant navy. I could describe others. It was intriguing to think of these men now in Salisbury, formerly as policeman, or ship's officer, or income tax officer.

All who become Christians need not leave their calling. For most, it is better that they should live as disciples of Christ in some business or profession. But with everyone a break is necessary. The break is, in fact, part of the individual Christian's basic experience. It is part of the Church's profession. The Church, the Christian, lives in the world, but there has to be the break *from* the world and *with* the world. 'Come, follow me', said Christ to Matthew, and he left all to follow. That is the picture to be set before every Christian. It is the experience baptism symbolizes, a basic experience to be lived through. So a right question to ask of all who profess to be Christians is, 'Have you experienced this break?'

2. *The re-association*

The break does not, however, issue in isolation. The Church is not the fellowship of the broken-away ones. It is not a retreat, not a cave for the separate. The break becomes a snare if it leads to separatism, the technical term for which is Pharisaism. Notice in today's Gospel that Matthew broke away at the words 'Come, follow me', but he re-associated himself with his fellow tax gatherers in the party he gave. Jesus was there. So Jesus called Matthew away to follow him, but both Jesus and Matthew re-associated with the people from which the break had been made. The break, therefore, is temporary. Clearly, the Christian is not to be '*of* the world', but he is to be '*in* the world', mixed up in its troubles and its joys. Such is the significance of the 'great feast' in today's Gospel.

3. *The proclamation*

The call of Matthew, his break with the old life and his re-association with his fellows provoked comment. In this there was made possible the proclamation of Christ. He was one who did not separate himself from sinners, he had come to heal them. The separation of the Church from the world and the involvement of the Church in service to the world constitute the twin foundations of the pulpit from which the righteous yet gracious Christ can be preached. At the moment the fashion is to stress the involvement of the Church, but if the separation is not also stressed, no preaching will be possible for long.

APPLICATION

St. Matthew speaks to us chiefly because he left all to follow Christ, but neither for separatism nor for sectarianism does his story give us any form of encouragement. Yet the break there must be.

SAINT MICHAEL AND ALL ANGELS

Angels

I would like to talk to you about angels. And you think the whole subject fanciful and me, the preacher, unrealistic, and the Book of Common Prayer with its St. Michael and all Angels' Day grossly unscientific. But I believe in angels, angels in heaven and angels on earth, and I do so because I have a particular belief about God the Lord of angels, and I submit this whole view of life enriches it beyond compare.

1. *God's messengers*

Let me put it this way first of all. Belief in angels is another way of saying that people and things can become the messengers of God to our souls.

I remember one night feeling jaded and tired, unable to complete the piece of work on which I was engaged. And then I heard the Adagio Movement of Beethoven's fourth symphony. That was God's angel to me. It, or the angel, or God, or both, gave me all I needed that night. . . .

And can't you remember months of sojourn here in London: and then you went out, out into the country, perhaps abroad. And the world seemed so still and the sky so blue, and the air fresh—God didn't seem so far off then. You could almost feel his presence—don't you know what I mean?

> Angels to beckon me
> Nearer, my God, to thee,
> Nearer to thee.

Am I wrong in this interpretation? But you can examine the Biblical use of the word 'angel' and as well as its application to celestial beings, its precise meaning is 'God's messenger'. You remember that magnificent scripture in the last book of the Old Testament, 'Behold, I send my messenger and he shall prepare the way before me.' That word, 'my messenger' is the same as for 'my angel'. It is the word 'Malachi', the name given to the whole book.

And so in the light of that I can *name* some of God's angels to us—people, solitary acts of kindness when you feel yourself in the desert of forsakenness, artists, musicians, the birds, that blackbird that sometimes sings in Cambridge Place; the flowers in the park, the touch of someone's affection when you're down.

> Angel voices ever singing
> Round thy throne of light,
> Angel harps for ever ringing,
> Rest not day nor night;

All these things can be God's messengers bringing new strength, new cheerfulness, new beauty, new bouyancy: the world is full of angels if only we always had the eyes to see. . . .

2. *Helpful powers*

And then in the second place the belief in angels implies the belief that there are powers to help us as well as powers to drag us down. We hear so much about the disintegrating forces of life. And sometimes Church people harp on these so much you wonder that they consider life worth living at all. There *are*, of course, wild beasts in life, there are wild beasts inside the human personality; we guessed this long before Freud told us about the 'Id' and the 'libido' down below the level of the human consciousness in every individual. And there are forces which would tear people apart; greed, lust, envy, bitterness—but there are also angels. Do not forget the angels.

I think one of the most striking phrases in the New Testament is in St. Mark's Gospel recording Jesus' temptation, his loneliness and his sojourn out in the wilderness. And this is what Mark wrote—'he was with the wild beasts, and angels came and ministered unto him'.

Yes, and life is like that. There are temptations. There are deserts to cross, even for the son of God. Then we are with the wild beasts, but the angels are there too, if only we will let them minister as Jesus did. 'And, behold, angels came and ministered unto him.'

It would take a long time to go through even a summary of the ministrations of angels as they are given in the Bible, they are so many; but let me hint at a few. Elijah, 'dead-beat' under a juniper—'Oh God, take away my life; for I am not better than my fathers. And behold, an angel touched him, and said unto him "Arise, eat". And he looked, and behold, there was at his head a cake baken on the coals, and a cruse of water.' Who was the angel? Some man? Some woman? Some shepherd? Does it matter? It was God's angel all right—it was the ministry of God's care for his servant exercised through a messenger.

And here is Peter, St. Peter in prison. And only if you've never been inside prison yourself can you fail to be interested. But who hasn't? Even of God's saints? The prison of depression —(life isn't worth the candle), the prison of constricting fear, the prison of self-centredness. And you can't get out. You think you'll never get out, but God sends his angel and you do get out, you scarcely know *how* you get out—that is the strangeness of this psychological experience—but a piece of music does it, or a talk with a friend, or a walk in the open is God's angel. 'God sent his angel and delivered us out of the prison.' Now go and read Acts chapter twelve . . . .

And here is Joseph, father of the holy family, perplexed about Herod, but the angel of the Lord guided them to Egypt. God's messengers are the counsels of friends, pastors, circumstances and the very scriptures from which we take our material. God's angels provide, deliver and guide in the wilderness of life. There *are* the wild beasts, but there are also the angels. . . .

3. *Colour in life*

And thirdly, I submit to you that this belief in angels relieves all the flatness of existence. There is of course, duty in life, cold, grey duty, and the rational element, and the abstractness of science—oh how I wish those girders being erected across the road could be left as they are, then I could say—look friends, that is science, it shows you what is the underlying structure of things, but is that all you need in life? Don't you want some plaster, some gay plaster? Don't you want to hang some pictures on the walls? Oh yes, there is science, engineering, thermodynamics and hydraulics—all very necessary, all very right and proper—but don't we also need the angels in life, angels of beauty, tenderness and the sheer illogicality of love? Oh what a relief to the flatness of life they make. I couldn't help thinking of that last Sunday afternoon as I sat in a train at Bradford Exchange station on my journey home. No angels there—but weren't there? There were for two lovers I watched just opposite my platform. . . . Oh I'm glad we have representations of angels up there in our church, and angels in gold on the reredos above the altar. I wanted the angels with trumpets high up above the organ gilded for all the congregation to see, but I'm told they can't be reached—we need to be lifted above commonplace thinking, we need to be reminded of angels. . . .

But the precondition of all this glory is faith, faith in the living God, faith in the God who cares for individuals, provides for individuals, guides individuals, and therefore employs messengers or angels to do it. Atheism and agnosticism always seem to me to produce drabness, whereas faith produces colour. So let us keep our faith alive and the angels *will* be seen, and if sometimes they look like ordinary men and women, don't be at all surprised. I could show you from the scriptures that the angels were often mistaken for men . . . and you never know, and this will surprise you, if not shock you, you might be an angel yourself this week to someone who needs you. . . .

SAINT MICHAEL AND ALL ANGELS

The advantage of innocence

St. Matthew 18.10 *'Take heed that ye despise not one of these little ones; for I say unto you, that in heaven their angels do always behold the face of my father which is in heaven.'*

1. Poetry

There are people who wish for no poetry in life. They see no sense in it. To them it is 'airy-fairy'. What they want is solid down-to-earth 'matter-of-factness'. Very well, but they must recognize how much they miss. There are some things you cannot catch without poetry; the blackbird's last song before the sun sets on an early summer's day, a child with curly golden hair racing across the golden sands to touch the gentle waves with all but ecstacy. Legal language is useless here, and so is science. You must have music or a poem, with all the inexactness those basic forms demand.

So if you wish to speak of man's relationship to God, scales are useless, rulers are useless, so are equations and statements verifiable by analysis. You must resort to poetry, and in poetry the angels come.

2. The access of angels

In old Hebrew thought there was an idea that a nation could have a guardian angel—Israel, Persia, Greece. In the book of the Revelation in the New Testament we read of the 'angels' of the Churches, that is, their representatives or their guardians. And in the Gospel for today 'the little ones' have angels who never fail to see the face of God in heaven; rather like court officials with constant access to the royal presence.

3. The access of innocence

What is the lesson here? What is the meaning of this poetic imagery of the children's representatives being in God's presence? Simply this, but profoundly this (which is why prosaic prose will not do). Innocence gives us access to God. The drift from innocence separates from God. This is why Jesus said, 'Blessed are the pure in heart, for they shall see God.' So the 'little ones' in today's Gospel are not only children but adults who 'with pure hearts and minds' follow Christ. It is easy for the worldly-wise, sophisticated in their *savoir faire* and *savoir vivre* to smile at them and call them 'green'. But there are advantages in the childlike (not childish) attitude to life, not least that it gives continual access to God's presence. It is what we seek in the Holy Communion. It is the reason we need confession and forgiveness before we draw near, for we must come as little children, it is the only way of spiritual entry.

SAINT LUKE THE EVANGELIST

A physician of the soul

2 Timothy 4.11 *'Only Luke is with me'*.

I wonder if you like your doctor? I hope so, because he won't be able to do much for you unless you do. But whether you like him or not doesn't wholly depend on you, it partly depends on him. Some people are easy to like. Others not so easy.

Now St. Paul was fortunate. He liked his doctor. Everybody liked him. He was so likeable they always referred to him by a nickname—Luke. In fact we do not know what his real name was. It might have been Lucius or Lucianus. But people used his name so often they couldn't bother to say all that, so they just said 'Luke' just as we might say Bill instead of William, or Penny instead of Penelope. It was a term of endearment. Everybody liked Luke. In his letter to the Christians at Colossae, Saint Paul wrote 'Luke, the beloved physician'. What volumes the phrase would tell if you heard it in this form in an English village, 'Charlie, the adored doctor'.

Now Luke was the man who wrote our third Gospel. He is depicted here on this balustrade* by one of these figures. I don't know if he looked like that, nobody knows, but I am quite certain everybody who knew him would agree that he ought to have a statue somewhere, they liked him so much.

Perhaps you are a little surprised to discover that the writers

---

*The balustrade of the pulpit where this sermon was preached.

of our first Gospels weren't all Apostles. St. Luke wasn't even ordained. He was a layman. He was a doctor. And that ought to stop us straight away from thinking there cannot possibly be any significant ministry for us in the Christian Church if we aren't ordained, if we belong to some other profession.

And what was it that St. Luke did for the Christian Church? He did three things.

(a) He put his professional skill at the service of the gospel.

(b) He, a professional man, became a friend to all.

(c) He wrote a book which bears his name, and probably another, the Acts of the Apostles.

1. *First of all, he put his medical skill at the service of the gospel*

What in fact this meant for him was accompanying St. Paul on his missionary journeys. Paul, you see, was liable at any time to be prostrated by some shaking disease, perhaps epilepsy. I have some sympathy! Very early on in my ministry I contracted from somewhere some disease in the blood, the effect of which was to cause me to run a high temperature with a rigor at half-an-hour's notice. More than once it put me in an awkward predicament. Thank God, it wore out after a few years. But I can sympathize with St. Paul. It was most embarrassing to be incapacitated by a shaking fit as he was when he first visited Galatia. The inhabitants were expecting a giant, and they saw instead a shaking, sick man. To help him, then, Luke accompanied Paul wherever he went.

Isn't there a lesson here for us? I know some already put what they have at the Church's disposal. I think of the number of eminent doctors who, here in London, give their services freely to St. Luke's Nursing Home for Clergy, for which I have personal grounds to be thankful. There are people here who have put their flat at the disposal of the Church for the furtherance of its work. And everyone who has some special skill and helps the Church along that line is doing what St. Luke did so long ago. We don't only need preachers and priests. We need laymen who support with their own special gifts the work for the furtherance of the Gospel. Money is not all we need. We need service. 'Luke, the beloved physician.'

2. The second contribution of St. Luke was friendship

'Dear old Luke.' Everybody liked him. I sense (I may be wrong), but I sense that he was not a great talker. He was, I think, one of those professional men whom the need for accuracy in his calling did not allow him to spill out words, wild words, unexamined words in every direction, on all occasions. He thought before he spoke. And you thought before you spoke to him. He could be disarming with his smile, but he could be debunking too. I am quite sure St. Paul, who steamrolled over most men, respected him. When the Apostle got carried away with one of his sweeping arguments there would be St. Luke, smiling, weighing it all up, wondering how all this grandiose array appeared in a practical setting.

But Luke never stole from you. He never stole your own sense of your own worth. He never demolished you with a smart saying, and then strode away leaving you hurt. He always stayed with you. He stayed with Paul in prison. His was always the gift of friendship to you. And that friendship was all the more striking because Luke was so cultured, perhaps *the* most cultured layman in the early Church. We can catch a glimpse of the kind of people who were his friends when he addresses the book to 'most excellent Theophilus'. St. Luke shows us what it means for a cultured person to be a Christian. It means keeping your culture, but being friendly to all who call themselves Christians. There are some who forget this. They forget that fellowship is the mark of a Christian, willingness for fellowship. Let St. Luke remind us of this today. Dignified, educated, cultured though he was, he was friendly to all. 'Luke, the *beloved* physician.'

3. His third contribution was to write a book

Many other Christians had tried to write an account of Jesus, but Luke wasn't satisfied with them. He agreed an account of

Jesus of Nazareth was necessary. It was all very well for St. Paul to propound his great doctrines of Justification by Faith and Sanctification and Election, but what most ordinary people need is a person to love and admire and follow. And so Luke, who understood people, determined to write that book. His was going to be an accurate book. He says he traced the course of all things accurately from the first. He asserts that his is an orderly account. He points out that his purpose is so that enquirers who have been taught only by word of mouth can read and examine for themselves.

And what a book he has given us! He wrote as much as one of those old manuscripts would take without starting another scroll. He wrote with a delicate touch. He presented Jesus as a human figure. He somehow elicited from someone, perhaps Mary herself, the facts, the strange facts, the intimate facts about the birth of her first-born child. And there is the parable of the Prodigal Son, the Good Samaritan, the Ten Lepers; everything tender and beautiful and compelling, St. Luke incorporated into his book.

And this is what we need to remember. We can't be instructed Christians without a book. Luke knew His Excellency Theophilus would have to possess a book if his faith was to be grounded. Your faith, my faith will not be grounded merely by hearing sermons, or any kind of hearsay. We must read the book. All Christians must possess the book, and read the book, and know the book.

The Christian faith was taken to parts of the west coast of Africa long before the nineteenth century, but none of these Christian communities survived because those early missionaries did not take the book.

This is what St. Luke teaches us, to ground our faith by means of a book. Notice how I phrased it. I did not say, ground our faith *in* a book. I said, ground our faith by means of a book. Our faith is in Christ, the man who is God for us. We believe he shows us how to live. We believe that by means of our trust we are enabled to live more closely to his pattern. But we shall never be kept to this belief and this life unless we have to read and study, a book. That is what St. Luke tells us on this, his day. 'Luke, the beloved physician.'

APPLICATION

St. Luke was a doctor. Have you some service you can put at the disposal of the Gospel? What are you actually *doing* for the faith?

Are you a friendly Christian, the very opposite of aloof? St. Luke, the cultured Christian is a reminder to us all.

Does the book play its proper place in your Christian life? You have little security of faith without it.

SAINT LUKE THE EVANGELIST

Why Saint Luke wrote

Luke 1.3 (NEB) '*And so I in my turn, your Excellency. . . have decided to write. . . .*'

But isn't that rather bold? I mean, isn't it rather bold to sit down and write a book? It takes time to write a book. It takes courage to write a book. Once what you have to say is committed to paper, you open yourself to criticism. You can't deny what you've written. You can't remove from other people's scrutiny every word you've penned. And what if a number of other writers have covered the same ground before? What makes you so certain that *your* book is required? And what about your public? You call him 'your Excellency'. 'And so I in my turn, *your Excellency*, have decided to write.' Is what you have to say likely to make an impression on a man or a class of person who obviously is educated, occupies some place of standing in the world and is recognized by a title? Luke, aren't you rather bold in writing your book?

Perhaps it isn't out of place to allude to the fact that I, the preacher, have written about ten books, and when publishing day arrives, and the reviews begin to appear in the journals, I always suffer a sinking feeling. Who am I to write a book? What do I know more than anybody else? Will someone tear my work to pieces and leave me wondering how I had the effrontery to produce it?

1. Saint Luke wrote history

I see St. Luke in his preface justifies himself. He says he has gone over the whole course of events about which he is writing in detail. In other words, he appeals to the diligence of his own research. In doing so he hints that perhaps those others who have taken upon themselves to write up the story he is about to write, might have done well to take a little more trouble. What then St. Luke says in effect is—'I know what I am writing about, your Excellency.'

Perhaps St. Luke had seen some of those government men from Rome thumbing through the other accounts of the early Christian story that had been produced. Perhaps he'd overheard those sharp-eyed legal gentlemen crying out—'O piffle! Can't be! Look, on this page he says this, on that page he says the other.' And the book was tossed into the waste-paper basket or the pending file, which is sometimes almost the same destination. And St. Luke thought—'If only I could set down pen to paper, I'd show them how true it is. Jesus *did* live. The Jesus who said and did the things reported was a real man in Galilee and Judaea. Here, give me the ink-horn! Give me the parchment!' and so St. Luke begins—

'And so I in my turn, your Excellency, as one who has gone over the whole course of these events in detail, have decided to write a connected narrative for you, so as to give you authentic knowledge about the matters of which you have been informed.'

Surely the first point that we can make about St. Luke's Gospel is that its author was firmly convinced in his own mind that what he was writing was history. After such a preface, with such a reader in mind, it is not likely that he would have included in his book fables and mythology, otherwise he would have made himself appear either a knave or a fool, or what is worse, both at the same time.

2. *It is the historic Jesus that makes men think about God*

Secondly, why did Luke write out this story? He was a doctor, a medical man. And if he was sufficiently broad in his approach to observe that when people have bodily ailments, it is wise to see them as whole persons, because what a man has on his mind may be as much responsible for what happens to the body, and vice versa. Why not then simply filter into people's minds ideas like 'God is love', 'God is a father', 'There is always a silver lining', 'Truth is great and will prevail'? Why bother with history? Why produce a connected narrative at all?

And St. Luke would answer rather disarmingly at first, I think, and simply say, 'Because it happened. I wrote all this because it actually happened. I checked the details.'

But there is more to it. St. Luke had travelled far and wide with St. Paul in the cities of the Roman Empire. There was beauty in plenty in those cities, but also filth in plenty. And religion was widespread. And philosophical discussion till there were scarcely any words more that could be used. Just like today. Men will talk about religion even if they will not believe in religion. No-one need worry while the talk lasts. No-one need take it too seriously. No necessity to do anything so long as it is only a matter for discussion. But suppose, just suppose that in the reign of Caesar Augustus a man was actually encountered of whom it was said that he came back from the grave! Would not the questions force themselves forward? Where? How? Who? What was he like?—That is why St. Luke wrote his Gospel. You can't simply write God off as 'airy-fairy' if what is reported of Jesus is true. The existence of God has to be taken seriously. St. Luke knew that even His Excellency Theophilus would have to take it seriously. That is why he wrote his book. That is why he wrote out his story in most careful detail.

And the pressure exerted by the history of Jesus has always existed. We have evidence of it in recent months not far from this church; Pasolini's film, *The Gospel According to Saint Matthew*. At a time when organized religion is not popular, night after night people have been queueing up to see a black and white Italian film with English sub-titles, made by a Communist, in the Paris-Pullman Theatre, Drayton Gardens, to the astonishment, I guess, of the management, who in consequence kept it running for weeks. The fact is, Jesus of Nazareth teases people's minds. Can he be true? But if he never existed, who thought him up? Who could possibly have invented him? But if he did exist, then our whole outlook on life has to be changed.

I expect you know that at the present time there is a cliché going the rounds which asserts that God is dead. What it really means, of course, is that the *experience* of God has 'died on' people. He is dead to them. And more than a few people are alarmed at how widespread is this human assertion. Even the *Times Literary Supplement* last week, a paper which cannot possibly be said to accord religion priority, had as its opening sentences, 'To judge from what has happend to language and thought since it was supposed that God no longer exists, it seems clear that he will soon have to be re-invented. Otherwise thinking persons are in danger of dying too, of boredom or inanity at the echoing rhetoric which the idea of so divine a decease too readily inspires.' And in a less rarified atmosphere than the world of letters we might similarly wonder how the stealing, cheating, drug addiction and promiscuity can possibly be checked so long as it is reckoned that God does not exist; and how is it possible to make people aware of him at all unless something did actually happen in the reign of the Emperor Augustus Tiberius which simply cannot be measured by a human yardstick. The fact of Jesus is the probe to our this-world viewpoint. How can we explain *him*? That is why Luke the doctor took up his pen and wrote. That is why he laboured to make it accurate.

APPLICATION

And if what I have said hangs together, if I have summarized accurately the past history and the present predicament, what more important conclusion is there at St. Luke's tide than to ask ourselves if we as Church people take sufficient trouble over examining our New Testament. In the end, I doubt if security of faith is possible apart from a grasp of this small book. The appeal has point especially for people at the level of His Excellency Theophilus. It was especially for such that St. Luke wrote. I do not think that we in a parish such as this can avoid the obviousness of the lesson. We ought to be doing more New Testament study. We ought to take the Bible Reading Fellowship seriously. We ought to respond to plans that will be suggested to form a study group. St. Luke wrote to give authentic knowledge. Only on a basis of authentic knowledge will faith stand firm. Only with a firm faith shall we rise in the twentieth century to our full humanity.

SAINT SIMON AND SAINT JUDE, APOSTLES

Contending for the faith

Jude verse 3 '. . . *ye should earnestly contend for the faith which was once delivered to the saints.*'

1. *The arena*

The television screen and the newspapers have been all but dominated by the 'coverage' given to the Olympic Games; and every Saturday afternoon there is ample opportunity for watching a sports contest of some kind. Perhaps we are not interested; or maybe, if we caught a glimpse of the sports arena with its struggles and exertions, it is the last experience we should choose for ourselves. But if we are Christians there is a struggle in which we must not shun participation, it is the struggle for the faith.

At all times there is a temptation for Christians to exercise their own faith and forms of worship in peaceful isolation. It is as if we say to the world, 'you go your way and I will go mine, leave me alone and I will leave you alone'. So the Church becomes a kind of ghetto, and Christians develop ghetto-like minds. And not even the technical theologians are free from blame. What is called Barthianism has resulted in a kind of non-engagement with 'natural' knowledge.

This does not mean that Christians are to be obnoxiously aggressive, but it does mean we are not to run away from argument and sticking up for what we believe. Remember Jesus. No-one can say that he let his opponents walk over him; on the contrary, quite often he beat them to a standstill by his dialectal skill in argument. Christians must not run from the arena of faith defence.

2. The treasure

In this short verse there are one or two technical words. One of them is hidden in the word 'delivered'. It is the Greek word παράδοσις. It occurs nine times in the New Testament. It means something which has been handed down, a sort of treasure or precious possession passed on from generation to generation. Christians could lose this. They have to fight to keep it. And the seriousness of the matter is that it was given 'once and for all' (see Jude verse 3 NEB). This is represented by another technical word, ἅπαξ. The truth is the faith can be philosophized away unless we contend for its historical root which is God come in flesh, the man Christ Jesus. Everything turns on the Incarnation, the Cross and Resurrection. If we do not contend for what has been given in these events we stand in danger of losing all.

3. The saints

We call today a Saint's Day, and so it is. It is not wrong to interpret a saint as some outstanding servant of God. But there is another meaning and it is the meaning most usual in the New Testament. The saints are the ordinary members of the Christian Church. What we are to understand, therefore, is that to all of us is committed the precious possession upon which our faith is built. We are all to fight for this. We are not to reckon that any of us can rightly opt out of the conflict. It is true some may have more weapons and bigger muscles for contests than others, but not all have to take on the same sized opponents.

APPLICATION

The Epistle of Jude might be called a 'tough' little letter. But we need it. We need to be reminded of the fact that the Christian Church has never been, and never will be, without opponents. Our duty is to contend. We must not run away. We have a treasure worth defending. It is our responsibility to pass it on intact to the next generation.

SAINT SIMON AND SAINT JUDE, APOSTLES

They also ran

I wonder if you are a talkative person? I wonder if you are the kind who can always be relied upon to fill the gaps in a halting conversation? The sort who helps to make a party go? Or who rises quickly to his feet at a public meeting? Our Lord had an Apostle like that. He chose him; chose him perhaps partly on account of his ready speech which can be useful. This was St. Peter. But not all the Apostles were like St. Peter. I bring to your attention today one who as far as the Gospel records are concerned, only spoke once, and that was to ask a question showing his ignorance. This was St. Jude, or if you want the old name—Judas, for there were two Judases in the Apostolic band, the one I bring to your notice today, and Judas Iscariot.

But it is not so much I that have brought this man Judas to your attention, but the day. If you look in your diary you will see that this is St. Simon and St. Jude's Day. And it is all too appropriate that we should think about these men, because although this church is dedicated to the Trinity, the nave and choir and south aisle were dedicated on St. Simon and St. Jude's Day 1903. In a sense these two men belong to us.

1. *Men in the background*

But why are they bracketed together? Why St Simon and St. Jude? The answer is because we know so little about them. They were numbers ten and eleven in the Apostolic list. Men at the bottom. Men who scarcely ever spoke, men of whom no great deeds are recorded. But they were Apostles. Christ chose them.

We might think about this for a few minutes. Christ chose for his Apostles some who by reason of their temperament would always stay in the background. Christ does not only call the extroverts. He has room for the shy and sensitive. And they have their work to do. Perhaps it does not hit the headlines. Perhaps a great deal of it goes unrecorded in the chronicles of the world. But Christ noticed St. Simon and St. Jude and singled them out, quiet though they were, to be his Apostles. So God notes that private act of kindness you did last week, that quiet Christian steadfastness in your office, that simple yet costly refusal of yours to become involved in some situation that would be contrary to your faith. On this St. Simon and St. Jude's day, let us notice that God does not overlook men in the background, and deeds done in the background. He has a place for people who are shy.

2. *A place for hotheads*

And now let us look a little more closely at the man Simon, number ten in the Apostolic band. There were two Simons, as there were two Judases. Simon Peter and Simon Zelotes. It is the second of these we think of today—Simon Zelotes, the Apostle after whom that small Church off Sloane Street in Chelsea is named. It is a rare dedication. And for this reason. We scarcely know anything about Simon Zelotes. He is not recorded as having said one single word in all the time of his company with Jesus. And yet he must have said something!

But there was nothing profound, nothing arresting, nothing significant.

Yet the fact that he was in the Apostolic band is striking. The suffix to his name 'Zelotes' means that he had been a member of the political party called the Zealots. These were hotheads. A group with no patience with gradualism. They wanted revolution at once. Drawn swords and general uprising. They wanted the Romans thrown out of Palestine by their necks. They couldn't wait for prayers and righteousness and God's intervention. How, with all that background, Simon came to be a member of the Apostolic band is remarkable. How he didn't come to blows with the other Apostles, and they with him is more remarkable still. And how, with all this impatience burning inside him, he never spoke up in the Apostolic band for his words ever to be recorded is one of the strangest facts in all the Gospels. What power Christ must have worked in this man! What power Christ must have worked in all his Apostles that they lived together without falling completely apart from one another.

When Arthur Foley Winnington Ingram was Bishop of London, the Diocese was more torn than it is today between the High Church and the Low Church. But the Bishop would never believe that the rents were there. And they weren't, of course, when he invited a High Church Vicar and a Low Church Vicar to talk things over in his study. All was perfect harmony. But the reason was the Bishop's radiant presence; no-one could fall out while he was there.

Was it, I wonder, something like that in the Apostolic band, with Christ's presence—John was reconciled to Peter, Matthew and Thomas and Simon Zelotes to Bartholomew.

Yes, St. Simon Zelotes has something to say to us. Christ has room for impatient people in his Church. He wants us there so that we may learn to live with other people. We shall learn it in his company.

3. *A place for the shy*

And now thirdly, I come back to this man Jude—St. Simon and

St. Jude. He spoke once. And then not till the night before our Lord's passion. And then to ask a question showing his ignorance. 'Judas (not Iscariot) saith unto him, "Lord what is come to pass that thou wilt manifest thyself unto us and not unto the world?"'

It was an elementary question, and yet I'm glad he asked it. I'm glad because it is a question dozens of us might like to ask but dare not. How is it that God has made himself known to us, but apparently not to thousands of other people? How is it that the majority of Londoners will not go near a church today, will not even think of eternal questions, will apparently have no desire to strengthen their hold in any kind of way on what we consider to be the final ground of all existence? How is it that God has made himself known to us, and not to all these other people? That was Jude's question. Jude's *only* question. 'What is come to pass that thou wilt manifest thyself unto us and not unto the world?'

And this is what our Lord answered. 'If a man love me, he will keep my words; and my Father will love him, and we will come unto him, and make our abode with him.' God is known to those who open their lives to his influence. The condition is on our side, not God's side. God wills to manifest himself to all who will receive him. Christ did not go in and out among the good people in Galilee, but amongst all people, right living and sinners alike. God is manifest to the man or woman who does not refuse to do his will in the ordinary affairs of life. Jude, are you listening to me? It is the human heart which conditions whether or not God is known; and a broken and a contrite heart he will not despise.

APPLICATION

Is your name Simon? Are you Zelotes? Do you rush to extremes? Does restraint sit uneasily on your temperament? God has a place for you in his Church, but you must hold that place with both your hands.

Is your name Jude?—a quite, shy, retiring individual. You,

too, are wanted. There is a ministry that is yours. And some will be thankful that you have a place within Christ's Church. They will adhere to you and not be frightened clean away for the simple reason you are there.

St. Simon and St. Jude! They also ran, though men never trumpeted their fame. Yet they were *with* Christ, and they *are* with Christ now in 'the realm where the spirits of the just are made perfect'. What a thought for All Saints tide. What an encouragement it brings. God has work for people in the background. They, too, will sit on thrones. . . .

ALL SAINTS' DAY

Lift up your hearts

Revelation 7.9 '. . . *a great multitude which no man could number*. . . .'

That is *not* what we see today. At least, that is what we keep on saying we do not see. We see only small congregations. We see statistics of declining numbers. We see ourselves as a minority movement in this secular age, which, in some of its aspects, is full of secular hope, promise and advancement, so our vision now is full of tiny totals, and we comfort ourselves, and maybe rationalize our situation by harping on the fact, which undoubtedly is true, that quality and not quantity is more important in the end.

But the seer in the scripture we read at All Saints' tide, in a passage from the Revelation, sees 'a multitude which no man could number'. And not only was he impressed by its size, he was impressed by its completeness. With that Hebrew mind which he possessed, how could he more emphatically press this point, than by sealing its number as a hundred and forty-four thousand, twelve times twelve times a thousand, and every twelve the multiple of three or four. That, to a Jew, was completeness indeed. Everyone was there, and when they were there, the total crowd was staggering.

And you think him fortunate to live in such a rosy time, to be able thus to think of Christian congregations forming such a vast assembly. But I remind you that this seer was eating out his heart in isolation in the slate mines on the Isle of Patmos. Chained, maybe, in a workgang, bruised and beaten by the foreman's leaded whip. No Christian fellowship on Sundays. No recognition of another Christian, except by secret signals with the fish sign. What chance for him to see a future for the Christian Church, other than sheer obliteration? He'd die himself ere long in the bitterness of labour camps, and not even a cross would mark his one and only resting place, a resting place in death. But instead, this man on Patmos saw 'a great multitude which no man could number, out of every nation, and of all tribes and peoples and tongues, standing before the throne and before the Lamb, arrayed in white robes, and palms in their hands . . . saying, "Salvation unto our God which sitteth upon the throne and unto the Lamb." '

1. *The wholeness of the Church*

Why can we not see this? Why are we whose lives are set amidst evidences of Christian triumph, why are we so beaten down by the smallness of our numbers? Perhaps we do not see the wholeness of the Christian Church. Perhaps we do not recognize the Christians out beyond our personal circle. Perhaps we have never really grasped the meaning of our Lord's own resurrection.

Let us look at these points. Perhaps we have not grasped the wholeness of the Christian Church.

It is an old and almost hackneyed story now, but I used it myself the other day to reset my perspectives. The vicar returned to the vicarage from an early morning celebration, where there had only gathered five or six communicants, and his wife, out of genuine sympathy for him, bemoaned the fact there were so few, but he replied, 'Only five or six that you could see, my dear, but I was reminded of the others when I read ". . . therefore with angels and archangels, and with all the company of heaven, we laud and magnify thy glorious Name; ever more praising thee, and saying: Holy, holy, holy, Lord God of hosts, heaven and earth are full of thy glory. . . ." '

We need to remind ourselves that the Church on earth is not the whole of the Church that is. There is the Church militant here on earth, and the Church triumphant, now in heaven. It is one and the same Church, though in two parts. This is the complete Church to which the Book of the Revelation, with its Jewish symbolism points; and when we look at the complete Church, it is a vast array numerically, 'a great multitude which no man could number'.

The seer of the Revelation had little material on which to build a vision when he saw it. A tiny Church remaining still in Rome, perhaps trembling under the persecuting hand of the Emperor Domitian. Could he have known that in 1578 a man digging near the Via Salaria outside Rome would open up a cemetery of Christians in which were buried six million (as Father Marchi says), how his faith would have risen then!

No, the Christians are not a tiny minority when we think at All Saints' tide of the whole and undivided Church. That thought can lift us up today, and send us on our way rejoicing in the great communion of diverse peoples.

2. Christians outside our circle

Why are we so beaten down by the paucity of numbers? Perhaps we do not recognize the Christians out beyond our personal circle. Perhaps there are more saints in Caesar's household than we have ever dreamed of.

Sometime less than a year ago I picked up a taxi in Kensington where I live, to take me on to Waterloo to catch a train. Now London taxi-men do not, as a rule, bother much with passengers, except to make sure the fare is paid, and a substantial tip is added on. And if the passenger happens to be a clergyman, even less attention then is given, perhaps due to anxiety about the tip. But my driver talked to me. All along Knightsbridge he talked, past the Palace, along the Mall, over Westminster Bridge. He wanted me to understand that he believed in God, and was himself a man of prayer. And when I paid him off at Waterloo, (plus a tip, gratefully received), we shook hands, to the evident surprise of the porters, but after all, it was only one disciple of Christ greeting another in the great Metropolis, a London Vicar and a London taxi-man, all saints, saints in Caesar's houshold.

You do not know who all Christ's disciples are, and nor do I. Sometimes they turn up in unexpected places. The cashier in the bank in Rome this spring, suddenly confessed to me he was a Protestant Church man. The business executive last month in the train to Birmingham, opened up on the meaning of our life. If only we knew all those in whose inmost heart of hearts there was a secret longing for the Christ of God, we would see, I think, what John saw on the lonely isle of Patmos, 'a great multitude which no man could number, out of every nation, and of all tribes and peoples and tongues', and then we should not be so downcast as we so often are.

3. *The meaning of the resurrection*

Why are we so beaten down by the poverty of numbers? Perhaps because we have not grasped the meaning of our Saviour's resurrection from the dead.

In his book *Faith in a Secular Age*, Colin Williams tells of how "in 1964 some negroes went to celebrate the three-hundredth anniversary of the landing of slaves in the United States of America at the site of the first slave market in St. Augustine, Florida. They held a rally proclaiming their right to participate to the full in the emancipation begun so long ago, and not yet complete. Hemmed in by angry whites, they demonstrated in open declaration of their rights, holding a 'wade-in' at the segregated beach, and singing and praying as they walked through the streets to witness their freedom. The whites threatened them, guns were directed at them; but they marched on. They risked death—and I asked one of the leaders why. His answer was that they believed in the resurrection. And that meant *now*, both because this new life in Christ demands to be shown forth as the life that transcends black and white, barbarian and Scythian, bond and free; and because this life cannot be broken by death. Those who die as they participate in the struggle are not left by the roadside by those who walk on to the final goal."

Perhaps this solidarity achieved by Christ is something we do well to recall when we think of loved ones we have left behind. They are not still in the cemetery. They are not really left behind at all, they have, in fact, gone on. Indeed, they are way ahead of us, knowing more than we, understanding more than we can ever hope to plumb with all our cleverness and skill. The barrier behind does not exist since Christ broke down the parting walls of death. The barrier is in front, in front for us; and when we, too, go through it, we shall be united in the one great multitude which no man can number, the Church in heaven, which is marching on.

Let us, therefore, at All Saints' tide lift up our hearts. Let us lift them up unto the Lord. The Church of God is not defeated.*

ALL SAINTS' DAY

Peace of mind

Some time ago there was brought to my notice a man who was bent on making a 'pile of money', and it had to be admitted that he was being successful. But when I observed his harassed face, and his nervous tension I caught myself uttering a kind of sigh. 'Oh how wretched are those whose lives are spent in the continual fight for money. . . .'

1. *The Beatitudes are comments on life*

Perhaps it is in some such way as this that we can best appreciate our Lord's use of the word 'blessed' in what are called 'the Beatitudes'. The Beatitudes are not theological statements or propositions. They are comments, almost passing comments, on ways of life. 'Oh the happiness of those people who have

* Published in *The Expository Times*, October 1966, and reprinted here by kind permission of the Editor.

learnt how to do without, they already know what the kingdom of God is like.'

It is important to notice how Jesus begins. He does not lay down the law. There is no 'thou shalt not'. The Sermon on the Mount in Galilee is not like the Law-giving on Mount Sinai in the desert. Nor does Jesus speak theoretically. Here are comments from observation of life itself, penetrating observation, observation of real people moving about in Tiberias, Capernaum and Jerusalem. Jesus saw what constituted peace of mind or blessedness. It wasn't possessing but being. It wasn't something in the pocket but something in the mind. This is the ground of contentment.

2. What takes away blessedness

Perhaps we could see more clearly what things contribute to peace of mind by considering what disturbs the mind. Geoffrey L. Heawood in his book *The Christian-Humanist Frontier* lists eight mental attitudes which correspond with their opposites in the Beatitudes. They are:

(*a*) Wanting what you haven't got.
(*b*) Self-pity.
(*c*) Wanting more appreciation.
(*d*) Boredom.
(*e*) Being misunderstood.
(*f*) Internal conflict.
(*g*) External aggression.
(*h*) Fear.

None of these makes a person blessed or happy, experience peace of mind, or whatever the word Jesus used (μακάριος) precisely means, but we know in our bones!

3. The characteristics of the saints

This is what all the saints have, all the saints in heaven. They have blessedness. They have peace. Not inactivity, not idleness, but contentment in living and doing and being. And all the saints on earth have it potentially and some all but have it actually, you can tell by their faces. Neither must we forget who the saints are, they are all who confess Christ's name. And this, of course, is the secret of contentment. It is to be in communion with Christ 'the Son of the Blessed'. It is what we seek at the Lord's table today. And when we come away, his blessedness should have been more deeply realized in our experience and perhaps even be apparent in our persons. It is blessedness that distinguishes the saints.